OSPREY COMBAT AIRCRAFT • 11

B-24 LIBERATOR UNITS
OF THE PACIFIC WAR

OSPREY
AVIATION

SERIES EDITOR: TONY HOLMES

OSPREY COMBAT AIRCRAFT • 11

B-24 LIBERATOR UNITS
OF THE PACIFIC WAR

Robert F Dorr

Front cover
On occasion, Liberators in the Pacific War were caught up in extraordinary actions – chasing Zeroes, or dodging phosphorus bomblets dropped by Japanese fighters – but for the most part the B-24 simply endured difficult maintenance and flying conditions, spanned enormous distances, and dropped its bombs. Artist Iain Wyllie has depicted this final task being accomplished by the natural-metal *Lil' Nilmerg* (B-24J 44-40861) of the 529th BS/380th BG. From this angle, the rather complex bomb-bay door arrangement of the Liberator is clearly exposed.

This bomber's unique nickname was reached by spelling the word Gremlin backwards, *Lil' Nilmerg* toting up the rather extraordinary achievement of flying 83 consecutive missions without a mechanical turnback. Constantly nurtured by a maintenance team under crew chief M/Sgt Valentine L Huck, the bomber actually survived the war and was scrapped in the United States on 1 May 1946

Dedication

This book is dedicated to the memory of John Lance, who flew B-24 Liberator missions as a pilot with the 23rd BS/5th BG 'Bomber Barons'

First published in Great Britain in 1999 by Osprey Publishing, Elms Court, Chapel Way, Botley, Oxford, OX2 9LP, UK

ISBN 1 85532 781 3

Edited by Tony Holmes
Page design by TT Designs, T & B Truscott
Cover Artwork by Iain Wyllie
Aircraft Profiles by Mark Rolfe
Figure Artwork by Mike Chappell
Scale Drawings by Mark Styling

Origination by Valhaven Ltd., Isleworth, UK
Printed through Bookbuilders Ltd., Hong Kong

99 00 01 02 03   10 9 8 7 6 5 4 3 2 1

EDITOR'S NOTE
The editor is keen to hear from any individual who may have relevant photographs, documentation or first-hand experiences relating to B-24 crews, and their aircraft, of the various theatres of war. Any material used will be fully credited to its original source. Please write to Tony Holmes at 10 Prospect Road, Sevenoaks, Kent, TN13 3UA, Great Britain.

ACKNOWLEDGEMENTS
Any errors in this work are the responsibility of the author. Assistance in the preparation of this volume was received from these B-24 Liberator crew members: Jim Cherkhauer (pilot, 531st BG/380th BG); Don Davis (radio operator/gunner, 494th BG); Harry Eberheim (gunner, 86th CMS); Roger Ellis (engineer/gunner, 424th BS/307th BG); John Farrell (pilot, 319th BS/90th BG); Phil Gowing (pilot, 400th BS/90th BG); Sterling Hays, mechanic (VPB-111); William Ray Hughes (navigator, 431st BS/11th BG); Rudy Liebsack (radar/gunner, 431st BS/11th BG); Tom McCarthy (radio operator, VD-4); Bob May (pilot, 11th BG); Stephen J Novak (90th BG); Bill Trash (531st BS/380th BG); and Ted Williams (navigator, 531st BS/380th BG)

Thanks also to: Allan G Blue, Bill Bartsch, John M Campbell, Michael English, Jack Fellows, Wally Forman, M O Freeman, Dan Hagedorn, Jim Harvill, William Hess, Dave Klaus, Tom Kolk, Kathryn Lance, Alwyn T Lloyd, David R McLaren, Sam McGowan, Clive A Lynch, David W Menard, Ian Quinn, Dave Ostrowski, Mack Peterson, Ronald R Sathre, John Stanaway, Jim Sullivan, Norman Taylor, Kirsten Tedesco, Bob Tupa and Martin P Winter.

CONTENTS

PEARL, PANAMA AND PARAMUSHIRO

It was not exactly a routine aircraft movement when 1Lt Ted S Faulkner departed Hamilton Field, in northern California, on 4 December 1941 at the controls of the third Consolidated B-24A Liberator (40-2371). Faulkner climbed into a dark sky, set throttles, and aimed his bomber toward Hickam Field, some 2400 miles (3862 km) away on the island of Oahu, in the Territory of Hawaii.

A member of the 88th Reconnaissance Squadron (RS), and head of one of two crews uprooted from Fort Douglas, Utah, by special orders a month earlier, 1Lt Faulkner had been assigned to a special and secret project to photograph Japanese installations in the Marshall and Caroline Islands, including Ponape and the Jaluit and Truk atolls. Although most eyes were on the war in Europe, many in the Air Corps – Faulkner included – believed that Japan might make a hostile move. The likeliest place was the Philippines (though the Japanese might be reluctant to commit their forces after the US completed its plan to station four bomb groups there by April 1942). It was equally possible that Japan might make aggressive moves out in the western Pacific where Faulkner was headed.

Faulkner had been commissioned during the lean years of the Great Depression. He was a quiet, competent man with a lean face and a small moustache, living in an era when even a mere lieutenant was given enormous responsibility. Although his squadron was equipping with shiny new B-17E Flying Fortresses fresh from the Boeing plant in Seattle – some of them would follow Faulkner's route to Hickam Field two

The Consolidated B-24 Liberator was the most numerous military aircraft ever manufactured in the United States, but it seemingly was mired forever in the shadow of the slower, shorter-legged, less numerous B-17 Flying Fortress. The men who fought in the Pacific theatre needed the speed, range and flexibility of the Liberator, but never shared recognition with their brethren in the Eighth Air Force. This rarely-seen photo depicts the first XB-24 prototype (39-556, later serialled 680) flying with gear down on an early test sortie from San Diego's Lindbergh Field (*Consolidated Vultee*)

In 1995, the manufacturer of a consumer product paid for a marketing survey to determine the 'most recognised' aircraft in history. To the dismay of B-24 Liberator veterans, their aircraft did not make the list. The Boeing B-17 Flying Fortress was at the top, ahead of the Douglas DC-3, the Boeing 747 and the Supermarine Spitfire. This B-17G (43-48111) is at Boeing Field in Seattle making a September 1944 test flight. The survey produced B-17 Steak Sauce, but no one can remember any consumer product having ever been named for Consolidated's heavy bomber (*via Norman Taylor*)

The very last 'Lib' to serve on active duty with the US Air Force was this Ford EZB-24M (44-51228), which participated in postwar icing tests and was finally retired in 1953. For almost half a century, this Liberator has been on outdoor display at Lackland AFB in San Antonio, Texas, where enlisted airmen – the author included – receive basic training. In 1998, the EZB-24M was slated for shipment to the American Air Museum at Duxford Airfield, in England (*Robert F Dorr*)

evenings later on 6 December 1941 – Faulkner had been on detached duty with the newly-formed Ferrying Command flying B-24As. He was well qualified for his secret assignment in the Consolidated bomber.

Faulkner was in the Army. To forever confound historians, the Air Corps remained as a combat arm of the United States Army which, after 20 June 1941, assigned its aerial formations to the Army Air Forces (AAF). That last term was always plural, and never accompanied by a 'US' prefix. Faulkner was a member of the Air Corps, but groups, squadrons, aircraft and bases belonged to the AAF.

Faulkner believed his photographic mission would help the United States prepare for war. The second photo project crew was also from the 88th except for the pilot, 1Lt Harvey J Watkins, who was from the 11th Bombardment Squadron(BS), 7th Bombardment Group (BG), also at Fort Douglas. Back at home base, the 11th BS/7th BG was equipping with factory-fresh B-17Es, too. It would have been inconceivable to any member of the 11th BS that within days they would be uprooted from Utah and would be in Arizona exchanging their new-smelling B-17Es for a less aesthetic aircraft called the LB-30.

Although the B-17 would later be one of the 'most recognised' aircraft in history – together with the DC-3, Spitfire and Boeing 747 – the aircraft in Faulkner's hands would remain forever a 'lesser-known'. Never mind that it was manufactured in greater numbers than any other US combat aircraft. The Consolidated B-24 Liberator (by other names the LB-30, F-7, C-87, C-109 and PB4Y-1) has become even less known today. Curiously enough, those who flew the B-24 may have helped. Some men swear by it. But some are like 1Lt Roland Stumpff, an instructor in both bombers, who remembers that, 'I flew the B-24 with contempt', and 'it

was a love-hate relationship'. The B-24 flew some of the most daring missions of the war, and flew farther and carried more than any comparable bomber, but outside the circle of those who love it, the B-24 never rated enough respect.

Nor has recognition been given to those who slogged in the Pacific theatre of operations – in reality several theatres, a sprawling expanse of a major proportion of the planet, with differing weather, climate and conditions, all of it difficult. Harry Eberheim, who flew with the 86th Combat Mapping Squadron (CMS), looked back later and recalled the 'lack of information about the Pacific operation versus Europe or Italy. I have always felt that because of the heat, health conditions, food and living conditions being so hard on one's body that we all just wanted to get it over with and go home. There was absolutely no glamour attached to service in the Pacific.'

B-24 INTRODUCED

Compared with the 7366 Lancasters and 12,731 Flying Fortresses which poured from the Western industrial machine, no fewer than 19,276 Liberators were built. This figure also exceeds production totals for Dakotas, Mustangs, Thunderbolts, Mitchells and Marauders. Liberators rolled off production lines operated by Consolidated (in San Diego, California and Fort Worth, Texas), Douglas (at Tulsa, Oklahoma), Ford (at Willow Run, Michigan) and North American (also in Dallas, Texas).

At one base in the American Southwest during the war, Liberators were parked wingtip-to-wingtip as far as the eye could see, stretching off the end of the airfield and out into the desert. 'We were building them faster than we could muster pilots to fly them overseas', a veteran remembers. 'You could look out, and there was no end to the sight of Liberators heading toward the horizon'. With a handful of exceptions, all Liberators in the Pacific came from the San Diego factory run of 7500 aircraft.

This great bomber owed strength and success to a unique wing sold to Consolidated in 1937 by a near-destitute inventor, David R Davis. Although the president of Consolidated, Reuben H Fleet, was sceptical at the time of the inventor's claims, wind tunnel tests showed that Davis's slender wing with sharp camber provided superior 'lift'.

The prototype XB-24 (the manufacturer's Consolidated Model 32) shined in natural metal when it first went aloft at San Diego on 28 December 1939. With war under way in Europe, the LB-30 export Liberator came ahead of US versions and contributed to their development.

This B-24A Liberator (40-2376) is a sister-ship of 1Lt Ted Faulkner's aircraft (40-2371) which was struck by Japanese bombs at Pearl Harbor on 7 December 1941 to become the first American aircraft destroyed in World War 2. Both aircraft had the US flag on the nose, the pre-war national insignia with a red circle in the centre (indistinct in this photo), the Ferry Command badge on the aft fuselage and a two-digit number on the fin. One of Faulkner's crew members recalls that the Ferry Command markings were retained on 7 December 1941, even though the bomber was slated for a secret reconnaissance project in the Pacific. The B-24As were painted in the early RAF camouflage of dark earth and dark green over black undersides (*via Dave Ostrowski*)

1Lt Ted Faulkner's B-24A Liberator (40-2371) is a distant image (second aircraft from the left) in this line-up of Ferry Command aircraft at Bolling AFB in Washington, D.C. months before the Pearl Harbor attack. Most A-models stayed with what became the Ferrying Division of Air Transport Command, and a couple of them carried out crucial evacuation missions during the early 1942 fighting in the Philippines and Java (*via Allan G Blue*)

As for the XB-24, it was powered by Pratt & Whitney R-1830-33 engines rated at 1100 hp apiece. In March 1939 the US Army ordered seven YB-24 service-test bombers with turbo superchargers for high-altitude flight. Next came nine B-24C models, none of which saw combat, and the B-24D which fought everywhere. The turret-equipped B-24H model, appeared on 30 June 1943, followed by the B-24J, which had full gun armament, including nose turret.

In the Pacific, the Japanese kicked the Americans out of Java despite a valiant battle by LB-30, B-17E and A-24 Dauntless pilots. Not until months later did the 90th BG 'Jolly Rogers' of the Fifth Air Force set up shop at Iron Ridge, in Australia, in November 1942, and move soon after to New Guinea.

Gen George C Kenney was a firm believer in the 'Lib', convinced that the B-24 carried more bombs than the B-17, had greater range, and could, if necessary, be flown seriously overloaded. No one ever claimed it was more elegant or performed as well at high altitude. But in rugged climes, where long-distance performance mattered – in short, in the Pacific – the B-24 became the right aircraft at the right time.

However, on the morning of 7 December 1941, 1Lt Faulkner's Liberator was most definitely not . . .

Lt Kunikiya Hira, leading No 3 Sqn from the Japanese carrier *Shokaku*, toggled the bomb release on his Aichi D3A Type 99 'Val' dive-bomber. His bomb - the first to fall on Hickam Field – hit Hangar 15 and set fire to the first US heavy bomber, probably the first US aircraft, to be

In the aftermath of the Pearl Harbor attack, Faulkner's B-24A lies in ruin at Hickam Field. All of these years later, a surviving crew member believes that the B-24A still carried the US flag on its nose and Ferry Command insignia on the rear fuselage, despite its intended reconnaissance mission. Examination of this photo with a microscope seems to confirm that the tail number '71' and the Ferry Command badge were still on the Liberator on 7 December 1941, but it may be impossible ever to be certain (*via Alwyn T Lloyd*)

destroyed in World War 2. It was Faulkner's B-24A, sitting outside the hangar and awaiting despatch on its photo Intelligence mission over certain Japanese mandated islands in the Central Pacific.

Two crew members were killed, three wounded – the first American casualties of the war. S/Sgt Burton R Grinyer, the crew's photographer, was walking toward the Liberator with two other members of the crew at the time of the attack. One of the men broke and ran, and was cut down by another Japanese aircraft on a strafing run. A second went in another direction and was wounded. Grinyer figured that lightning couldn't strike twice and dived into the crater made by the bomb. He survived unhurt. The AAF had just lost ten per cent of its B-24 inventory.

THE LB-30

Between 10 December 1941 and 6 January 1942, the USAAF took possession of 75 LB-30s. Six were lost in US accidents, 23 went to Britain and 46 served the US in various roles. The LB-30s that eventually went to Java with the 7th BG were flown only by the group's 11st BS. Crews picked them up at the Consolidated modification plant at Tucson, Arizona. After a hasty crew checkout, they departed for Wright Field, Ohio, for further modification, and from there to the port of debarkation – MacDill Field at Tampa, Florida – where they were processed for overseas movement and sent forth.

The AAF ordered the 11th BS (and the rest of the 7th BG with its B-17Es) to the Philippines, which was then succumbing to the Japanese onslaught. Some were routed across the Pacific through Australia, while others flew a route through South America, across Africa and India. Six crews of the 11th BS took the latter route, while the remainder travelled west.

In fact, it was too late to bulwark the Philippines. On 8 December 1941, towering incompetence on the part of Gen Douglas MacArthur caused much of the United States' airpower in the region to be caught and destroyed on the ground. By January 1942 the Philippines was being overrun. The 7th BG ended up instead on Java, where some hope existed of slowing the Japanese advance.

JAVA BATTLE

The 7th BG's first combat mission was launched on the night of 16-17 January 1942. Maj Austin Straubel (in AL609) led three LB-30s piloted by 1Lts Jack Dougherty (AL535) and William E Bayse (AL576). These Liberators, along with two B-17Es, took off from Malang and flew north-east, where they stopped overnight at Kendari, refuelled, and loaded bombs. Straubel, the flight leader, was the man everyone knew would rise to become chief of staff – he was tough but fair, competent but pleasant. It is difficult to believe that, today, no Air Force Base is named in his honour.

Straubel's bombers proceeded to two targets on Celebes – an airfield at Langoan for the LB-30s, while the two B-17Es struck at shipping in the harbour of Menado. These were the first combat missions flown by the B-17E model and by the LB-30, the first bomb mission in the Pacific flown by an outfit other than the 19th BG (B-17C/D), and the first in which any American aircraft had tail guns.

Maj Gen Clarence L Tinker (seen here as a colonel) flew everything in the Air Corps' inventory in the 1930s. At the time of Pearl Harbor, he commanded what later became known as Seventh Air Force. His loss during the battle for Wake Island in an LB-30 Liberator was an enormous set-back for the AAF. The general's name lives on at Tinker Air Force Base in Oklahoma City, Oklahoma, where many Liberators underwent depot-level maintenance and modification during the war (USAF)

Seen at Tucson, Arizona, in December 1941, this LB-30 Liberator (AL576) was piloted by 1Lt William Bayse, who flew an Atlantic route to reach Java early in 1942. Once intended for British use, the LB-30 bomber had hand-held guns in the nose, tail and amidships in a dorsal location. This was one of three LB-30s and two B-17Es that flew the 7th BG's first combat mission of the war. Americans on Java were overwhelmed within weeks (*Robert Graf*)

MINNIE FROM TRINIDAD (AL608) was the only LB-30 Liberator from the 11th BS/7th BG to escape to India after the Allies were routed from Java. Capt Horace Wade flew *MINNIE* from Jogjakarta to Ceylon on the evening of 25 February 1942, carrying British Gen Sir Archibald Wavell and other officials to safety. The 7th BG later fought in India and the Middle East in B-17Es, before returning to the China-Burma-India Theatre in B-24s – but never again the Pacific (*L B Clemans*)

'When we took off', remembered Straubel's, bombardier, Capt Raymond O Carr, 'we had to use our landing lights, as no runway lights were on. This field (Kendari) was the objective of the Japanese who had landed, so we fully expected they were already around the field and would start firing at us when they saw our lights. I had the .50-cal (12.7-mm) gun in the nose ready to shoot the minute I saw any sign of them. Nothing happened on the outskirts of the field, so we breathed a sigh of relief and began concentrating on the work before us.'

At Langoan, Straubel's flight bombed the airfield from 19,500 ft (5945 m), arriving over target at 0536. The men saw no aircraft on the ground. They noted no anti-aircraft fire.

'We didn't come in contact with any pursuits', Carr recalled. 'We took a straight course for home and slowly lost our altitude as we thought we didn't have anything else to worry about. Suddenly, somebody yelled, "Pursuits!" We were attacked.'

From 0609 to 0615, five Mitsubishi A6M Zeroes attacked the three LB-30s. One of the gunners was credited with shooting down one Japanese fighter. Aboard Bayse's bomber, 1Lt Victor Poncik saw Dougherty suddenly peel off to the right into a huge cumulus cloud with an engine smoking '. . . and we saw no more of him', although he was later to reappear.

Bayse's bomber took hits in two engines. He feathered one and shut it down. He struggled to keep formation with Straubel, but fell back, even at full power on the remaining engines. Finally, with two badly wounded gunners on board, with damaged flight controls and hundreds of miles yet to go to Java, Bayse elected to try to land at a Dutch airfield at Macassar in the south-western Celebes. He made an emergency crash landing. The wounded men were removed and taken to a Dutch hospital. The remainder of the crew was unharmed but the aircraft was, as Poncik put it, 'only food for salvage'. Eventually, with a Japanese landing at Macassar imminent, two Navy PBY Catalinas picked up some of the downed airmen, who took a launch out to the waiting PBYs while explosions and fires lit up the Macassar waterfront. Two weeks were to pass before a Navy PBY picked up the crew of Dougherty's LB-30 (AL535), which had ditched near the shore at Maselembo Island in the Java Sea.

Americans fought in vain against the Japanese tide in Java. The veteran B-17C/D-equipped 19th BG was all but decimated after being blooded in the Philippines. The newly arriving 7th BG, with its 9th BS at Madioen (B-17E) and the

11th BS at Jogjakarta (LB-30), struggled to put a handful of bombers into the air to strike Japanese airfields on the Malay peninsula and convoys in the waters nearby. The air commander, Maj Gen Lewis H Brereton – who, two months earlier, had been rebuffed upon urging MacArthur to disperse his air power in the Philippines – arrived in Java on 28 January 1942 aboard a Ferry Command B-24A (40-2373).

On the trip, he was buffeted by rough weather, a reminder that this was the worst time of the year to be flying. Brereton concluded that Java could not be held. The Japanese had now occupied the airfield at Kendari, and a strike by two LB-30s on the night of the 28th produced unknown results. Three LB-30s attacked a favourite target at Balikpapan two days later, ushering in the very grim month of February 1942.

On 72 hours into the new month, the 7th BG's beloved commander Maj Austin Straubel finished a meeting with Brereton at Bandung and took off in a 'hack' Douglas B-18 (36-338) to return to his embattled main base at Malang. A dynamic leader who wanted the 7th BG to make its own mark and not merely function as an appendage to the battered

The LB-30 Liberator bombers flown by the 11th BS on Java (seen here) and the 29th BS in Panama were manufactured with an open gun position and two hand-operated .50-cal (12.7-mm) machine guns. One tail gunner described the vertigo he encountered while his bomber was heading in one direction and he attempted to shoot at a Japanese fighter headed in another. A second gunner said the arrangement was relatively 'efficient'. On Java, several gunners were credited with aerial victories (*Robert Graf*)

Unable to hold Java against the Japanese onslaught, Allied forces abandoned the island in early 1942. Capt Elbert 'Butch' Helton and 1Lt Victor Poncik flew this LB-30 Liberator (AL515) out of Jogjakarta, Java, on 3 March 1942, evacuating the last American personnel to escape from the embattled island. One LB-30 took the 7th BG flag to India, but other survivors (including AL515) retreated to Australia, where they did not again play a significant role in the Pacific War (*Horace Wade*)

Since B-24D models came out of the factory wearing camouflage, a natural-metal D-model seems an odd sight in retrospect. But oddity was the norm in the Sixth Air Force, where bomber crews flew exhausting long-range patrols over the Pacific from bases in Panama and elsewhere in Latin America. Sixth Air Force veteran Col O C 'Ole' Griffith snapped this B-24D Liberator, with war paint removed, during a visit to Talara, Peru, apparently in 1944 (*Dan Hagedorn*)

19th BG, Straubel had hoped to sort out command arrangements and prevent his men and bombers from being squandered piecemeal in a poorly-planned campaign. He was bucking the tide. The brass at Pearl Harbor, and especially MacArthur in the Philippines, had utterly failed to make effective use of their men and aircraft as the Japanese pressed their attack. Now, Japanese fighters attacked Straubel's B-18 near Surabaya. Straubel and six others died as the B-18 spouted flames and plummeted to earth. Command of the 7th BG passed to Maj Kenneth Hobson.

On 3-4 February LB-30s flown by Capt Horace Wade (AL609) and Murray Crowder (AL533) ventured into Del Monte – the last US base in the Philippines – in a risky marathon trip (40 hours flying time in a 48-hour period) to deliver supplies and bring people out. On the 5th Lt Arthur 'Bud' Fletcher's LB-30 (AL515) attacked Japanese islands near Singapore. The 7th BG lost half a dozen B-17Es in the next few days while the noose tightened on Java, and the handful of LB-30s continued flying long-distance, often solo, missions. Four LB-30s took off from Jogjakarta on the night of 9 February and successfully bombed a Japanese vessel at sea, but the ship was not, as the men believed, an aircraft carrier.

On the night of 12-13 February three LB-30s took off from Jogjakarta to bomb Japanese ships in the vicinity of the Anambas Islands. The bombers failed to locate the vessels and returned from a fatiguing mission with no results. The men saw fires burning in Singapore in the distance, and that island fortress fell to the armies of Japan's Gen Tomoyuki Yamashita two days later. Closer to Java, the Japanese seized Palembang, the principal port on Sumatra, that same day. With Borneo, Celebes and Timor also under assault, the island of Java (which belonged to the Dutch) was the final Allied possession not yet in enemy hands.

On 17 February Brereton and Maj Gen George Brett decided to divide

More than half a century later, almost nothing is known about the small blurred symbols appearing on these 29th BS B-24Ds beating up Rio Hato, Panama, in 1944. The B-24D in the foreground (41-24063) carries the ASV radar antenna array found on Sixth Air Force B-24Ds and LB-30s during the war. The antenna is barely visible in the dorsal area on the spine of the Liberator and beneath each outer wing panel. 41-24063 survived the war in Central America and returned to the USA in July 1945 (*Dan Hagedorn*)

up the surviving forces in Java, with Brett taking US aircraft and crews to Australia, while Brereton would move to India to build a force to strike at Japan through China. Two days later, a trio of LB-30s bombed Japanese ships off Bali. Zero fighters attacked the formation at 3000 ft (914 m), and the bomber crews claimed two Navy fighters shot down, although Japanese records indicate only damage. A day later, an LB-30 bombed a Japanese destroyer off Java.

On 20 February three LB-30s of the 11th BS left Jogjakarta to again bomb Japanese ships off Bali. The flight was led by Capt Wade. He pressed the attack from 13,500 ft (4115 m) and each bomber dropped eight of the British 300-kg bombs the Americans had been using.

Wade's bombardier, Sgt Charles Schierholz, was certain they sank a Japanese cruiser. Bomber crews reported three direct hits and eight waterline hits on a cruiser which was left burning, but Japanese records do not indicate damage to *Nagara*, the only light cruiser assigned to Bali operations. Wade's LB-30 force encountered no Japanese fighters and heavy, but inaccurate, anti-aircraft fire.

LOSING BATTLE

Elsewhere on Java B-17s and a handful of newly-uncrated A-24 Dauntlesses were busy, but it was a struggle to keep the 11th BS's LB-30s in action, On 21 February two LB-30s again went after enemy ships in the vicinity of Bali, with newly-seized Denpasaar as a secondary target. One aircraft dropped its bombs on a tent camp, the other on what was apparently the airport, with no visible results. Records show that this was the 18th mission launched by LB-30s during the Java campaign.

A strafing attack on Jogjakarta the following day destroyed an LB-30 (AL567) on the ground and hinted that the Japanese would soon be able to overrun the embattled 7th and 19th BGs. That day, US Army chief of staff Gen George Marshall ordered Brereton to withdraw from Java.

Lt Crowder flew Gen Brereton and staff members from Bandung to Colombo, Ceylon, in his LB-30 (AL533) on 24 February. Crowder

returned to Java – and thereafter took his LB-30 to Australia – while Brereton went on to New Delhi to set up a new Tenth Air Force headquarters. In the weeks ahead, the 7th BG would relocate to India, but with B-17Es only, while many of its members would be absorbed by the B-17C/D-equipped 19th BG in Australia. Only much later, after a Mid East episode in Flying Fortresses, would the 7th BG return to the China-Burma-India theatre and operate four squadrons of B-24s.

Capt Wade and his crew flew *MINNIE FROM TRINIDAD* (AL608) from Jogjakarta to Ceylon on the evening of 25 February 1942, carrying Brereton's new boss, British Gen Sir Archibald Wavell and other officials. At Colombo, Wade picked up Gen Brereton and carried him on to Asansol, India, where the 7th BG had relocated with B-17Es.

Back in Java, the end was near. On the night of 27 February 1Lt 'Butch' Helton took off in an LB-30 to bomb Denpasar airport, on Bali. He bombed by moonlight at 1230 from 7000 ft (2133 m) and reportedly scored five hits with his 300-kg bombs. One sign of the chaos that now overcame the 7th BG's 11th BS at Jogjakarta was the carefully kept record listing aircraft serials and crews on particular missions, which abruptly ended the previous day.

On the night of 28 February 1942 one B-17E and one LB-30 launching from Jogjakarta combined with five B-17Es from Madioen to bomb

Ford B-24M-FO 44-51589 was devoid of unit insignia or individual artistry when it flew with the 29th BS (Heavy) from the Gallapagos Islands in April 1945. But this bomber wore the distinctive 'patrol' scheme that cloaked several of the late-war Liberators used on gruelling anti-submarine patrols in defence of the Panama Canal (*Charles Meketa*)

B-24D 41-23908 from the 21st BS was returning from a bombing mission over Kiska on 18 January 1943 when its home base at Adak became shrouded in fog. The crew made the difficult choice to belly-in on the tundra surrounding the volcano on Great Sitkin Island, just off Adak. The Liberator is reportedly still there today (*via Allan G Blue*)

Japanese ships just off the north coast of Java. As was frequently the case in these early, difficult missions, each bomber proceeded to the target individually. This was the 21st LB-30 combat mission. A day later, an LB-30 pilot had to bring his bombs back when he was unable to find the Japanese ships.

On 1 March a determination was reached that three LB-30s at Jogjakarta (AL533, AL572 and AL609) would have to be written off. Dutch soldiers began blowing up everything at the base and the evacuation got underway – four transport B-24As, a B-17 and an LB-30 hauled men and equipment out of Jogjakarta en route to Australia. Loaded to capacity, these aircraft made harrowing flights out of Java to the evacuation base at Broome, on the Australian north-west coast. The last two LB-30s got out on the night of 2-3 March, piloted by Crowder and Helton. Many ground personnel got out on a Dutch ship. But on 3 March the Japanese mounted a surprise air attack on Broome that destroyed two B-17s and three B-24As on the ground, whilst B-24A 40-2370, flown by Lt Kester of Air Transport Command, was shot down just off the coast from Broome, and all but one person aboard killed.

In the battle for Java, B-17s withdrawn from the Philippines had been joined by 39 more Flying Fortresses and exactly a dozen LB-30 Liberators. Of the 12 LB-30s that had reached Java and fought on that embattled island in those dark days of early 1942, only four survived. Seven aircraft (AL533, AL535, AL567, AL572, AL576, AL609 and AL612)

Lined up on the pierced-steel planking that defied mud, sleet and ice in the Aleutians, this crew of *KISKA KATIE* (41-23896) of the 21st BS is in a good mood because the men have just completed a combat mission. Their B-24D-10-CO Liberator was shot down during a later sortie near Attu on 15 May 1943 (*via Allan G Blue*)

The Japanese always constituted the main threat to Liberator crews, even in the sparsely populated Far North, but the weather always enjoyed a close second place as their ever-present nemesis. This khaki B-24D-15-CO (41-23973) is making its way above a fog layer near a mountain peak in the Aleutians (*via Allan G Blue*)

were written off and lost in action, whilst one other (AL521) was destroyed during a Japanese air raid on Darwin. Three LB-30 bombers (AL508, AL515, and AL570) went to Australia to join Brett's forces. A single aircraft (AL608, *MINNIE FROM TRINIDAD*) went to India.

HAWAIIAN AIR FORCE

Many thousands of miles from India where *MINNIE FROM TRINIDAD* exited the Pacific Theatre, the Hawaiian Air Force reeled from the Pearl Harbor attack, struggled to re-assemble itself, and confronted a losing conflict in the Pacific. In due course, the Hawaii-based air arm would become Seventh Air Force (see Chapter Three). But first loomed a losing battle for Wake Island, seized by Japanese forces which rapidly outnumbered American defenders.

Apart from the loss of Faulkner's bomber during the Pearl Harbor attack, no B-24 bombers had any role in this early fighting. But six LB-30 Liberators had arrived at Hickam Field in February 1942. They were not thought suitable for combat, but did participate in two bombing missions to Wake. Otherwise, they served as long-range transport aircraft, serving in the central Pacific virtually until war's end, operating a transport/cargo service dubbed 'Southern Cross Airways'. The name and concept were the work of one of the AAF's great pioneers of the previous decade, and the first wartime commander of the Hawaiian command, Maj Gen Clarence Tinker.

Japan's seizure of Wake Island was a dark moment for Americans. Midway, it was hoped, would be different. Although the LB-30s were not thought suitable for bombing, Tinker led four of them on a raid on 6 June 1942 off from Midway Island in a night bombing raid against Wake, now a Japanese bastion. The hope was that the Liberators would successfully bomb key enemy warships. Gen Tinker's LB-30 (AL 589), flown by a pilot with mostly single-engined qualifications, became lost and crashed into the Pacific. The remaining three LB-30s never found their targets. A second LB-30 strike on Wake was marginally more successful, but the loss of Gen Tinker was a stunning blow.

LIBERATORS IN PANAMA

There was only one other theatre where LB-30s flew combat missions. It was not, by most definitions, part of the Pacific War, but it involved a great deal of flying over the Pacific by men who were as dedicated as any in the conflict.

Defending the Panama Canal was the job of the Sixth Air Force, which operated fighter and bomber squadrons at several bases in the Canal Zone. As early as 28 February 1943, the little-known Sixth had 13 LB-30 and 22 B-24D Liberator bombers on charge, although the commander, Maj Gen H R Harmon, reported that his LB-30s had inadequate armament, unreliable bomb racks, radio and radar that could not operate simultaneously, undependable communications and electrical systems, and a host of other problems. The B-24Ds and LB-30s had been hastily equipped with ASV (Air-to-Surface Vessels) Mk II radars for maritime and anti-submarine patrol. Although drawn from Liberator stock intended for Britain, these American LB-30s appear to have been painted in standard AAF olive-drab camouflage. Beginning in 1944, the defenders of the Panama Canal began to receive a few more advanced B-24J Liberators, plus at least eight B-24Ls. At the very end of the war, 12 B-24Ms were added to the Canal Zone force. At one point, Sixth Air Force's authorised strength reached 62 Liberators.

B-24s belonged to the 6th BG, which included the 3rd, 29th, 74th and 397th BSs. These B-24Ds and LB-30s were equipped with British developed ASV radar, which included antennas beneath the outer portions of both wings and in the dorsal position ahead of the empennage. In addition, the 7th Radar Calibration detachment operated two B-24Ds. There were few examples of distinctive unit markings, unusual camouflage or nose art on these Liberators, although one LB-30 (AL640) dubbed *JUNGLE QUEEN* wore a nose caricature of a nude bathing beauty similar to those seen in other theatres.

This panorama illustrates the conditions faced by Liberator crews in the Aleutians – a Quonset, a flag flapping in the breeze (with stars for the 48 US states) and a seemingly endless expanse of ice. These are B-24Ds of the 21st BS (*via Allan G Blue*)

A Jeep was a must for getting around the dispersals in the Aleutians, as it offered a modicum of protection from the bitter weather. The driver of this canopied vehicle has pulled up in front of one of the huge revetments at Adak to check on the progress of engine maintenance being performed on the B-24D in the background. Although no mechanics appear to be present, the starboard inner engine is running well, and its opposite number on the port wing has its access panels cranked open (*via Allan G Blue*)

Typical was the 29th BS, which came to the Liberator only after a metamorphosis which involved earlier duties as a medium-bomber outfit (Douglas B-18s) and a brief time with only one aircraft on charge – an L-4 Cub! The squadron received its first three B-24Ds at Antenna, Panama, on 17 April 1943, and began sea patrol missions that encompassed an arc from Panama to Saloons, in Ecuador, and to Taker, in Peru. The squadron was deployed to the Galapagos Islands on 9 May 1943, and its B-24D strength peaked at nine aeroplanes.

It would be almost impossible to overstate the gruelling, difficult conditions under which the men of the 29th BS and other Liberator squadrons patrolled for German and Japanese threats. The nature and extent of the threat was unknown. Even today, it is unclear what the Japanese were doing on the Pacific side – the records of Japanese submarine operations in that sector of the ocean were later destroyed. But protection of the Canal was vital, and the men of squadrons like the 29th BS made an important contribution while they endured long hours of difficult flying, with poor navigation references, over vast stretches of ocean, and in littoral regions where the weather and terrain were often hostile.

The 29th BS moved to Howard Field, Panama, on 10 April 1944 and re-equipped with B-24J and L-models. Few records have surfaced from the final days of the war, and it is unclear how many of the later Liberators were equipped with the air-to-surface radar pioneered by B-24D and LB-30 crews. In fact, although there were armed engagements with German submarines on the eastern (Caribbean) side of the patrol area, it is thought that none of the Liberator crews ever engaged a Japanese vessel on the Pacific side of the Panama Canal.

WAR IN THE ALEUTIANS

Even less publicised than the Liberator crews in Panama were those who fought in the Aleutians. The 28th BG, originally a Composite Group, was the parent outfit for the 404th BS, which flew Liberators. It received little attention, but 28th BG Liberators bombed Japan's home islands as early as 18 July 1943. The Japanese naval base at Paramushiro became one of those perennial targets, often damaged but never neutralised. In addition to its bombing duties, the 28th BG specialised in photo and radar reconnaissance, as well as sea search and rescue.

The 404th BS/28th BG operated from Ladd Field, Alaska, beginning 12 July 1942, and from Nome Municipal Airport beginning later the same month. It carried out the dreary Aleutian 'thousand-mile war' with alacrity and great dedication, and at times the cold was a deadlier enemy than the Japanese. 28th BG flew 2578 sorties during the war, suffering 33 aircraft losses and receiving credit for 29 Japanese aircraft shot down. Twenty-two more Liberators were lost in non-combat mishaps.

FIFTH AIR FORCE

For a brief period in 1945 as the Pacific War drove relentlessly toward Japan's home islands, two of the premier American bomb groups were flying from the same base.

As Liberator crews neared the end of the long road that began at Pearl Harbor and on Java, the 90th BG 'Jolly Rogers' and the 380th BG 'Flying Circus' were sending their Liberators skyward from the same taxyways and runways. It was high drama for the Pacific region where, unlike Europe, the sight of large numbers of Liberators was uncommon.

The place was McGuire Field, San Jose, Mindoro, the Philippines, and the dates of overlap were from 20 February to 9 August 1945. Finally, B-24 Liberator crews were together in numbers. The growing numbers would be even more evident in the final weeks of the war when the 90th BG moved to Ie Shima to fly alongside the 43rd BG. By then, however, attention would shift to another bomber – the B-29 Superfortress.

The story ended with American bombers darkening the skies of Japan. But it did not begin that way. At the beginning, the Liberator's sturdiness on 'lone wolf' sorties, its long reach, and its ability to fly and fight in heat, dirt, grit and rain – often alone – were he stuff that made the Fifth Air Force. And in the early months, the 90th BG was the only Liberator group in the Pacific. 'I never saw a formation larger than three B-24s', says Phil Gowing, a 400th BS/90th BG co-pilot.

FIFTH AF BACKGROUND

The south-west Pacific was always the province of Fifth Air Force, the air command that came under Gen Douglas MacArthur's headquarters in Australia. So vast was the Pacific Ocean that B-24 Liberator crews flew in 'numbered air forces' in three principal regions. Here, in the south-west Pacific, two of them overlapped sufficiently to bewilder even an expert on geography.

Fifth and Thirteenth Air Forces were at each other's elbows. Early on, Fifth was responsible for New Guinea while Thirteenth held responsibil-

B-24D 42-41127 of the 90th BG 'Jolly Rogers' on an early Pacific combat missions. Early in the war, all of the group's squadrons used a black background on olive drab tails, and it was not until mid-1944 that the 90th BG received B-24Js and went to a natural metal finish with distinct tail colours for each squadron – red for the 319th BS, blue for the 320th, green for the 321st and black for the 400th. The lower nose shape depicted here is a Hawaiian Air Depot modification (*via John Stanaway*)

A nose turret-equipped B-24D of the 528th BS/380th BG makes a bombing run over a target at Amahai on Caram Island, in the Molucca Straits – part of the Netherlands East Indies – on 21 December 1943. The thin high-aspect Davis wing of the Liberator became a familiar sight to Japanese troops, some of whom saw it only when bombs were falling (via Allan G Blue)

ity for Guadalcanal, a scant 500 miles (805 km) away. Far away from both, way up in the central Pacific, was Seventh Air Force.

But because it rings with the name of Gen George C Kenney, Fifth Air Force will always be regarded by many as the premier Liberator outfit in the Pacific. Fifth Air Force leapfrogged forward against the Japanese in the New Guinea, the Bismarck Archipelago, Netherlands East Indies and Philippines. At the end of the war Fifth was moving to the Ryukyus for the invasion of Japan.

Once called, simply, the Philippines Department, Fifth Air Force received its name and number in February 1942, although Gen Kenney reorganised it after his arrival in July of that year. Few individuals in this century have had more influence on the outcome of a military campaign. MacArthur's biographer William Manchester said 'The importance of Kenney to MacArthur in the following three years cannot be overestimated'. When Gen Kenney took command of Fifth, he also assumed command of the Allied Air Forces in the south-west Pacific, including those of the Royal Australian Air Force (RAAF) and the Netherlands East Indies Air Force.

George Kenney was as leader as well as a commander, a man who inspired devotion from the young men he was sending into peril. The one factor that seems to stand out in regard to the airmen who served under him is that while they detested MacArthur, the airmen loved Kenney and were willing to lay their lives on the line to turn the tide of war in the

21

south-west Pacific. Kenney referred to his men as 'my kids'. His memoir of the war, *General Kenney Reports*, is full of anecdotes about the men who served under him – this is a reflection of his attitude toward his men, both officers and enlisted.

Kenney saw the B-24 Liberator as suitable for the Pacific at a time when the top brass in Europe were unhappy with it as a strategic bomber. Because his background had been in fighters and attack, Kenney was not hamstrung by the 'strategic bombing' ideas that characterised much of the Army. He was not out to prove a concept, but to drive the Japanese out of New Guinea and to retake the Philippines. Instead of insisting that his heavy bombers operate at high altitudes, he used them in low-level attacks on Japanese shipping, while strategic missions were flown at lower altitudes than in Europe, thus allowing the crews to achieve greater bombing accuracy – Pacific bomber crews were also able to operate at lower altitudes because they were crossing water, not hundreds of miles of land covered with flak guns.

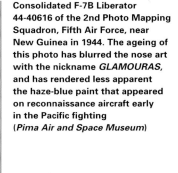

Consolidated F-7B Liberator 44-40616 of the 2nd Photo Mapping Squadron, Fifth Air Force, near New Guinea in 1944. The ageing of this photo has blurred the nose art with the nickname *GLAMOURAS*, and has rendered less apparent the haze-blue paint that appeared on reconnaissance aircraft early in the Pacific fighting (*Pima Air and Space Museum*)

Nearly all of the thousands of Liberator crew members had a photo like this during the war. This portrait, standing as a symbol for all the crew pictures in all B-24 squadrons, shows men who flew with the 319th BS/90th BG 'Jolly Rogers'. They are, from left to right, back row: John Farrell, pilot; Robert Conover, co-pilot; Al Rogan, navigator; Gerry Roenning, bombardier; Ed Jakubiak, engineer. Front row: Bob Dolitsky, radio operator; W Bolger, gunner; Usher Francis, gunner; Henry Bland, gunner; and Ed Badsky, second engineer (*John Farrell*)

As a commander, Kenney used his air units in a concerted effort. He encouraged the strong-willed, and often inaccessible, Gen MacArthur to adopt a strategy that used fighters to gain air superiority while the heavy bombers attacked strategic targets and the medium/attack bombers struck Japanese shipping and airfields, and used airlift to move the Allied positions further and further north as they drove the Japanese away from Japan. He also encouraged the bypassing of major Japanese troop concentrations, then used air power to isolate and render them ineffective. These tactics resulted in the lowest casualty rates of any theatre of the war.

Before Kenney arrived, the Allies were reeling from their staggering defeats at Pearl Harbor, Singapore and – despite the best efforts of the LB-30 Liberator-equipped 11th BS – Java. In this early phase of the fighting, much of the burden fell on the 90th BG. The group's commander, Col Arthur H Rogers, who gave his name to the group's 'Jolly Rogers' appellation, described his outfit as 'the first heavy bomber unit to reinforce a losing army in the jungles of New Guinea'.

THE 90th BG

The 90th BG (Heavy) was constituted on 28 January 1942 and activated at Key Field, Mississippi, on 15 April 1942. The group moved a month later to Barksdale Field, Louisiana, where it trained in B-24Ds. The 90th BG went to Ypsilanti, Michigan, in August 1942 for further training and engineering updates not far from the Ford plant. At the time workers at the site were on strike at the very time members of this Liberator group were preparing to go to war!

The group moved on 12 September 1942 to Hickam Field in Hawaii. Here, as a result of the stay adjacent to the Ford plant, the men modified their aircraft with various internal improvements. Here, Maj Arthur H Rogers and Col Marion D Unruh planned the installation of Consair A-6 tail turrets to the nose of the B-24D, which had been manufactured with glass noses and no nose turret.

While the 90th prepared for battle in Hawaii, a squadron commander and the group commander questioned the value of the B-24 Liberator – and, almost to the point of mutiny, demanded B-17s. On 8 October 1942, AAF boss Lt Gen Henry H 'Hap' Arnold wrote letters to Kenney and Hawaii-based Maj Gen Willis Hale of Seventh Air Force acknowledging 'a real and acute problem in psychology and leadership',

Consolidated B-24J-120-CO Liberator (42-109987) *PRETTY BABY* on a Pacific combat mission. With the exception of a few F-7 photo ships and a few C-87 transports (and also excluding the Sixth Air Force in Panama), virtually all Liberators in the Pacific Theatre of Operations came off the San Diego, California, production line, even though B-24s were also manufactured by Consolidated in Fort Worth, Douglas in Tulsa, Ford at Willow Run and North American in Dallas (*via Robert F Dorr*)

and confirming no change in his plan 'to replace B-17 type aircraft with B-24 type aircraft in all of the combat theatres throughout the world except the United Kingdom'.

Arnold noted that the Flying Fortress was 'a fine heavy bomber which has been lavishly built up by the press'. As the 90th BG headed to war, Arnold was concerned that the 90th was replacing the B-17C/D-equipped 19th BG 'with the general belief that their airplane (the B-24) is an inferior weapon'. Arnold noted that 'a number of pilots thoroughly experienced in B-17s' were then commanding B-24 units 'and showing real pleasure and pride (in) their new B-24 aircraft' – but not in the 90th BG, where a mutinous attitude prevailed.

While the 90th was still on his turf in Hawaii, Hale sacked the group commander (Col Eugene Mussett) and a squadron commander. He redressed a complaint of 'congestion' in the nose by having the navigator's position moved from the nose to a new location behind the pilot. And he oversaw the effort to install nose turrets in the B-24D aircraft. At the time, Arnold and others expected that the Liberator would eventually receive a 'Bendix' turret. He was referring to the 1942-era Bendix remotely-sighted 'belly turret', which appeared for a short while on the B-17E and the B-24D – it proved worthless and was removed. Later-model Liberators received MPC or Emerson nose turrets at the factory.

NOSE GEAR PROBLEMS

The B-24 was a far better aircraft than the true believers of the B-17 world would admit. But no sooner had the 90th BG arrived in Australia than the B-24 experienced a series of nose wheel failures. These were caused by faulty actuating cylinders which raised and lowered the gear. In the 'down' position the cylinder became a stress-bearing member, and the bolts used to fasten the ends of the cylinder to the gear and to the bomber were failing. The 'fix' was to replace these bolts with case-hardened, solid-shank eyebolts of much greater strength than the originals. This was one problem for which the remedy was quick, although some crew members continued to believe that the nose gear was weak.

On 16 November 1942 the 90th BG went to Iron Range – a location

"HELL'S BELLE" is a khaki B-24D on a mission near New Guinea. The wartime caption for this photo says that the Liberator has just scored a direct hit on a 5000-ton Japanese transport off Kairiru Island on the north coast of New Guinea. The vessel that can be seen beneath the fin of the B-24D does not seem to have suffered any damage, however (*via William Hess*)

The wind is blowing smoke skyward (upper left) from bomb hits at Namlea township airfield, Boeroe Island, in the Netherlands East Indies on 17 August 1944. A pair of B-24 Liberators of the 529th BS/380th BG 'Flying Circus' are pulling away from the target area (upper right) in this combat photo taken from the right waist-gun position of yet another B-24 (*via Allan G Blue*)

so remote no roads connected it to other towns in Australia. Here, field work finished the job of equipping the B-24D with a nose turret, which produced an unexpected benefit.

According to Maj Rogers, who evaluated the nose-gun installation when urged by Gen Kenney, 'I performed this test and was pleased to find out the airplane had actually picked up from eight to twelve miles per hour at the different settings. This had been due to the shifting forward of the centre of gravity, which made the airplane fly on an even keel. Before this, the plane had been tail heavy, and had a tendency to fly nose up, which increased the resistance and slowed down the speed. After completing these tests I was anxious to get back up North in the combat zone to actually find out the results of the nose turret against the Japs' head on attack.'

B-24 Liberators of the 529th BS/380th BG on a 1944 combat mission (*via Allan G Blue*)

A Fifth Air Force document from the era says that the Iron Ridge-based 90th BG 'entered combat immediately'. Japanese forces had landed at Buna and Goma on the north coast of New Guinea the previous July and at Milne Bay – the eastern tip of New Guinea – in August, Now, with inexperienced crews, the 90th BG began attacking Japanese airfields, troop concentrations, ground installations and shipping. By year's end, friendly forces had pushed the Japanese back over the Owen Stanley range and recaptured Buna and Goma, shifting attention to Guadalcanal and the main Japanese base at Rabaul, on New Britain.

Col Arthur Meehan (who relieved the hapless Mussett) was the first commander of the group during its combat duty in the south-west Pacific. He was lost in combat on 17 November 1942, and Col Ralph E Koon was named group commander the following day, with Lt Col Arthur Rogers as his deputy. Koon remained as group commander until 11 July 1943 when he was replaced by Rogers.

NEW GUINEA

The 90th moved to Port Moresby on 10 February 1943. The fighting was unglamorous, pushing the B-24 crews to the limits of their training, which, in Gen Kenny's view, had been inadequate. He noted that, 'This job here calls for night take-offs with maximum loads and often with cross-winds, climbing through overcast to 15, 000 and sometimes 20,000 ft to get on top in order to navigate. It is then normally necessary to come on down to see the target under a ceiling which may range from 2000 to 10,000 ft, pulling back on up after the attack to navigate home, and on arrival back at Moresby in breaking through again to land.'

As for New Guinea which was to be the centre of action for Fifth Air Force for two gruelling years, Lt Col Arthur H Rogers said, 'Just prior to

While Fifth Air Force bomber crews were slogging their way through New Guinea and other hellholes, the US Navy was preparing to introduce its own version of the twin-tailed Liberator to the combat zone. This Consolidated PB4Y-1P Liberator photo-ship belongs to one of the 'VD' (reconnaissance) squadrons that flew the type in the Pacific. This ship (BuNo 32308) was ordered as a B-24J-145-CO with AAF serial 44-40061 (*via Jim Sullivan*)

the War, I heard that a survey was made relative to living conditions in New Guinea, and the report that the committee made was that the one place on the face of the Earth that a white man could not live long was New Guinea. This I heartily agree with. Even if malaria, typhus, dengue fever, dysentery and all the parasitic diseases were completely blotted out, I still believe that the intense heat and miserable humidity would sap the strength of a white man in a few short years.'

Many of the missions consisted of two or three bombers, rarely even accompanied by a handful of the other diverse aeroplanes in the region P-39 and P-400 Airacobras, P-40 Warhawks and B-25 Mitchells.

The aircraft flown by the 90th BG were initially camouflaged (olive drab) B-24D models with standard serial-number presentation on the tail. Nicknames and caricatures began to appear on their noses at Iron Range, and were common at Port Moresby.

ENTER THE 'CIRCUS'

In May 1943 the 380th BG 'Flying Circus' joined the fray, becoming Gen Kenney's second B-24 Liberator formation. From Fenton and later Darwin, Australia, the 380th BG was to operate until early 1945 almost alone against airfields, installations, industry and shipping in the Netherlands East Indies, Timor Sea and Banda Sea areas. The 380th was to become a frequent visitor to Balikpapan, the well-defended Japanese oil refinery complex on Borneo. The group consisted of the 528th, 529th, 530th and 531st BS.

The newly-arrived 'Flying Circus' tested its mettle with a 23 June mission to Makassar, on Celebes, travelling 2000 miles (3220 km) and bombing docks and shipping facilities.

Meanwhile, at Port Moresby, the 90th BG acquired perhaps the

Seen earlier in this chapter, *"HELL'S BELLE"* receives attention from 90th BG mechanics, apparently at Port Moresby, in 1943 (*via William Hess*)

best-known nickname of any B-24 combat unit. Col Arthur Rogers assumed command of the 90th on 11 July 1943, and almost immediately after came a decision that would affect the image of 90th BG and create jealousy in other units of the Fifth Air Force. Col Carl Thursgard, the photographer for Acme Pictures (who was to die on a mission just days later on 20 July) was with another war correspondent visiting in the tent of Lt Bernard Stoecklein. The latter, from his long sojourn in Australia and privy to Col Rogers, had the talent always to have alcoholic libations available. After a few drinks, he remarked, 'We need a name. A good one'.

Since Rogers had just become commander, someone mentioned 'Jolly Roger'. The comment was about the person, but Stoecklein took it as a suggested nickname, was ecstatic, and could not wait to get Rogers' approval. He fixed the commander a drink and went next door to his tent. No sales pitch was needed – Rogers was immediately sold on the nickname.

Stoecklein, as group statistical officer, had on his staff an artist and draftsman in Sgt Leonard H Baer – who came up with the design similar to the 'Jolly Roger' of pirate fame, but with the skull grinning and the bones replaced with bombs. He cut out the design in plywood and painted it beneath the serial number on the tail of Col Rogers' aircraft, *CONNELL'S SPECIAL* (B-24D-5-CO 41-23765).

By September 1943 another Liberator group had joined Fifth Air Force, the 43rd BG 'Ken's Men' (named in honour of Gen Kenney) having finished their conversion from the B-17E/F Flying Fortress to the B-24. From October 1943, the group's 63rd BS served as a low-level night and attack pathfinder unit, using specially equipped radar bombers. The 64th, 65th and 403rd BS began their B-24 era with almost all of their Liberators in natural metal finish.

BIG MISSION

Although Liberator crews rarely saw mass formations in the Pacific, there were exceptions. The Japanese base at Rabaul drew American bombers and fighters like a magnet, and on 12 October 1943 Fifth Air Force sent 63 Liberators, 107 Mitchells and 106 Lightnings to Rabaul. More strikes followed. Low-level B-25 Mitchells did much of the work, but Liberators also struck from on high.

Remembered Col Rogers (with some words in his account omitted);
'Bougainville, north-west of the Solomons, was located right under the

GLORIA MARIE NEW ORLEANS **is one moniker that appears nowhere in a surviving record of nicknames assigned to 90th BG bombers. By 1944, the 'Jolly Rogers', who had begun as the only Liberator group in the South Pacific, were beginning to get plenty of company. As for the olive-drab paint scheme that had become so familiar, it had begun to give way to what is commonly, if somewhat misleadingly, called natural metal finish at around the same time (*via Robert F Dorr*)**

nose of Rabaul. The plan was to take Bougainville by an amphibious force from the Solomons, but as long as Rabaul remained the great naval and air power that it was, the chances were that our landing force on Bougainville would be wiped out before a firm beachhead could be established. In the great harbour at Rabaul (were) 50 to 65 ships anchored at all times. The air power varied from 400 to 600 planes on the four airdromes.

'The plan consisted of a co-ordinated attack of light bombardment, (with B-25) Mitchells, acting as strafers. Liberators, with only ten per cent of our fighter strength, would strike 45 minutes later, and what enemy fighters had not been destroyed in the air we figured would be back on the ground refuelling.

'I had had the camouflage paint removed from my plane *CONNELL'S SPECIAL*, and our aluminum surface was polished until she had become known as the "silver streak". I did this in an effort to prove that our camouflage paint was a detriment instead of an aid in both camouflaging the airplane as well as making it heavier, thereby slowing it down. The entire Air Force had come to the conclusion that it was impracticable to try to camouflage an airplane as large as a Liberator (Rogers was urged by crewmen to fly a different B-24, as the shiny silver was certain to attract Zeroes, they believed).

'A few minutes after (take-off), we assembled our large formation over the field and departed for the Tobriand Islands (where) our fighter formation was waiting for us. Our flight across the Bismarck Sea was uneventful with the exception of two airplanes in my formation having to return due to engine trouble. Our flight to within one-and-a-half hours of the target had been made at an altitude of approximately 13,000 ft (3962 m). This was done – even though our bombing altitude was set for between 20,000 (6096 m) and 24,000 ft (7315 m) – because a man cannot live above 15,000 ft (4572 m) without oxygen, and our supply of oxygen aboard each plane could not be depended upon for more than three hours.'

Rogers led his part of the formation into Rabaul as gunfire arched upward;

'As I glanced out to see which way to turn to evade the flak so that my entire formation would not be blown out of the air, I was amazed and

As the war progressed, the colourful 90th BG boasted a few Liberators that were without distinctive nick-names or caricatures on the nose. Much of the surviving pictorial record of the 90th BG is the work of a single photographer, Stephen J Novak, who carried a camera with him on combat missions, and took some of the best shots of the 'Jolly Rogers' in action (*Stephen J Novak*)

flabbergasted to see just ahead of us the biggest swarm of enemy fighters I had ever seen in the air at one time. About the same time, I was on my radio calling for help from our fighters, and from their own conversation it was evident that they were so outnumbered they were having a problem looking out for themselves. I never saw a one of our fighters after I commenced my bombing run.

42-41222 is a nose turret-equipped B-24D-50-CO of the 530th BS/380th BG 'Flying Circus', seen here over Maomere on 17 July 1944. Evident from this angle are the manually-operated ventral machine-guns that replaced the retractable ball turret on many Liberators in the Pacific (via Allan G Blue)

'I knew now something had gone wrong with the original plans and I wondered if the Mitchells were unable to reach their target since I could not imagine how it would be possible for the Japs to throw this many fighters at us if they had had a previous engagement. I could see Zeroes flying to pieces in front of us as our good old nose turrets rotated so as to keep the enemy fighters in our gun sights at all times. My plane had received a 20 mm shell in the left wing tank and the hole had been so large that the self-sealing material of the tank was allowing the gasoline to seep out. With the exhaust flame not far from the escaping gas, our plane became a fire hazard. I had to slow down since one of my wing men's engine had been struck and was belching smoke. From radio conversations the other flight commanders were all having their difficulties, and I began to wonder if any of us would get back. The Japs had followed us out 75 miles (120 km), and were still attacking us fiercely as if the fight had just begun.

'The Japs continued to dog us until we were 175 miles (281 km) out. All the planes in my flight had holes in them, but after conferring with the airplane commanders, I decided that none of my six planes (in Rogers' immediate flight) were damaged to the extent that we could not make it to (the staging base at) Buna. My navigator, Conti, was working furiously on his problem of navigation, since I had used many evasive manoeuvres during the 175 mile (281 km) running fight across the Bismarck Sea. He gave me a new course that would bring me into Buna, and after heading on this course for some 30 minutes, my aerial engineer informed me that our gas lost from the damaged wing tank was far greater than I had

Like so much that happened in an expansive and primitive theatre where men were busier swatting away mosquitoes than keeping records, no one seems to know exactly where or when this PB4Y-1 Liberator of VB-106 suffered this ignominious 'crack-up'. This diorama of twisted metal and broken aircraft was preserved on film by Vice Adm John T 'Chick' Hayward, who later pioneered the Navy's carrier-based nuclear strike forces in the 1950s (US Navy)

expected. It was a question then whether I could get to Buna or should I go back to the Tobriand Islands. I decided to try and make it on to Buna, and we arrived there all right. I notified the control tower to have the fire trucks and ambulance on the alert since it is impossible to determine how much damage has been done to a plane while it is still in the air. Oftentimes flak will puncture a tyre which is retracted up in the wing, cut a hydraulic line, or damage the retracting mechanism itself. Some structural member of the plane might have been damaged and so weakened that when subjected to the stress of landing it gives away, causing a crash.

'On approaching the field I proceeded straight in to land since my plane was running short of gas. A nice landing was made, but as the plane slowed down to within five and ten miles an hour (16 km/h) the nose-wheel strut gave way and we stopped just off the edge of the runway on our nose. Everyone crawled out, and after an inspection it was found that a shell had cut through the strut, weakening it, which caused the failure. Other planes landed and it was found necessary to leave two of them at Buna for repairs.'

1943 FIGHTING

The Allies were advancing now, and the 90th BG 'Jolly Rogers' were able to move to newly-seized Dobodura, New Guinea in December 1943, The year ended with the Allies beginning to wrest New Britain from Japanese hands. Now, Rabaul, that best-known of targets situated at the north-eastern tip of New Britain, would cease to matter.

The 20th CMS began operations in late 1943 from Port Moresby, and soon afterward from Nadzab, New Guinea, with the F-7 – the photo-reconnaissance version of the Liberator. The squadron's light-hearted emblem was the copyrighted *Yosemite Sam* character from the Warner Brothers cartoon films.

Modified by the Army Modification Center, the F-7A was based on the B-24J variant and carried three nose and three bomb bay cameras. The F-7B model had six bomb bat cameras. The configuration included K.17 Tri-Met (three cameras - port,
vertical and starboard, with an overlapping angle of photography by five degrees giving horizon to horizon coverage).

On 3 February 1944 58 B-24 Liberators and 62 B-25 Mitchells spear-

44-40395 wears the diagonal black fin stripe that identifies the 64th BS/43rd BG 'Ken's Men' on a sortie over New Guinea. The group's 65th BS had a pair of dice showing the numbers '4' and '3' in the same location on the fin, while the 403rd BS was distinguished by a black quartered square on the upper forward fin. Some aircraft carried the sobriquet 'Ken's Men', honouring Gen George C Kenney, on the forward fuselage (*via Allan G Blue*)

MAD RUSSIAN was a B-24M-1-CO
(44-41846) of the 65th BS/43rd BG
'Ken's Men' at Clark Field, in the
Philippines, on 1 June 1945
(*via William Hess*)

headed an assault on the airfields at Wewak. A week later, 48 Liberators
of the 43rd and 90th BGs, with P-38 Lightning escort, assaulted the
important Japanese airfield at Kavieng, New Ireland, north-west of
Rabaul. It was the beginning of a series of raids in which B-24s led the
way, sometimes assisted by A-20 Havocs and B-25 Mitchells.

'RED RAIDERS'

A latecomer to the Liberator armada in Fifth Air Force was the 22nd BG
'Red Raiders' that began flying B-24s at Nadzab in January 1944. By
then, the definitive Liberator was the B-24J, coming from the factory in
natural metal finish and bristling with guns. One old-timer greeted the
arrival of a pristine 'Red Raiders' J-model with the acerbic comment,
'Spiffy!' – perhaps unaware that the 22nd had been blooded in B-26
Marauders and B-25 Mitchells almost from the very beginning. The 'Red
Raiders' kicked off their Liberator era by attacking Japanese airfields,
shipping and petroleum in Borneo, Ceram and Halmahera.

Ultimately, the 'Red Raiders' of the 22nd BG were to fly and fight from
airfields at Nadzab, Port Moresby, Biak, Clark Field and Okinawa.

The 90th BG picked up stakes and moved again to Nadzab on 23
February 1944 (joining the 22nd BG and 20th CMS). Moving westward
along the northern coast of New Guinea, Allied forces were to bypass
Wewak and go after Hollandia. The first softening up attack on
Hollandia was delivered by 22 Liberators on 4 March 1944. Two weeks
later, as the Japanese withdrew from Wewak and concentrated at
Hollandia, 40 Liberators bombed shipping from medium altitude and
sank a freighter. Some 75 Liberators hit Hollandia on 30 March, 71 the
following day. These were huge raids for the conditions of the theatre.

Finally, on 22 April American troops seized Hollandia. The war moved
on. That week, 47 Liberators of the 43rd and 90th BGs bombed Biak,
claiming credit for three Japanese fighters downed in the air and 13
destroyed on the ground.

Phil Gowing, co-pilot in the 400th BS/90th BG, remembered a
nocturnal mission to Yap Island on 13 June:

'We took off from Nadzab in the morning and flew about three-and-a-
half hours to Mokerang strip, on Los Negros Island, to refuel. This was a

joint effort with the 43rd BG, and together we got 13 aircraft in the sky. Took off again at 2100 and got into the middle of a storm about two hours later. Six of the thirteen aircraft turned back, but we were too green and too stupid to turn back because of bad weather. There were no star shots that night, and we really didn't know exactly where we were.

'But when our ETA (estimated time of arrival) for Yap came around, we opened the bomb bay doors and let them fly. Our Radio Operator, Gene Sullivan, emptied his .45 (Model 1911 Colt .45-cal. automatic pistol) through the bomb bay also, shouting "Take that, you S.O.B.s". We saw a flash of lightning and of course had to report night fighter interception. I'm sure we did a lot of good that night, burned a lot of fuel, killed a lot of fish, wasted a lot of explosives, lost a lot of sleep. But to this day we tell Sullivan that he got two Japs with his .45. We finally landed at Hollandia at 0700, refuelled again and went back to Nadzab. That was the last mission for our Bombardier, who really lost it that night. After a month of psychiatric interviews, he was sent home. I often wonder who was really nuts, him or all of us.'

Asked about the long hours of boredom that were part of Liberator life in the Pacific, Gowing recalled, 'Our first mission was also our longest – 18 hours and 40 minutes'.

Throughout the long struggle to turn the tide, the 2nd Photographic Charting Squadron had done much of the photo work for Kenney, some of it in F-7 Liberators that began to replace earlier photo-ships in 1944.

In a major re-organisation on 15 June 1944, Seventh and Thirteenth Air Forces were merged into a single command, designated Far East Air Forces (FEAF). On that date, Lt Gen Ennis C Whitehead replaced Kenney, who was perhaps the most beloved combat commander of the war. Later, FEAF would also subsume Seventh Air Force in the central Pacific and, after the war it would also gain responsibility for Twentieth Air Force, which, during the war, had a handful of Liberators. Under the change, each numbered air force retained its distinct identity.

Fifth Air Force was destined to continue the fight as part of FEAF (see Chapter Five), but by then it could already boast a litany of achievement – the Fifth had halted the Japanese drive in Papua, recovered New Guinea, neutralised islands in the Bismarck Archipelago and the East Indies, and would soon help to liberate the Philippines. Most of the way toward Tokyo, the Liberator would continue to have plenty of work to do.

A Japanese fighter approaching from this angle would confront four .50-cal (12.7-mm) machine-guns from the dorsal and tail positions, plus perhaps a waist gun a moment later. The Liberator was also too fast to be easy prey when engaged from behind. This PB4Y-1 Liberator wears the national insignia that was in use prior to April 1943 (*via David Parsons*)

SEVENTH AIR FORCE

The Seventh Air Force was at the forefront of the American drive in the central Pacific at the very time Fifth and Thirteenth Air Forces were tied up in the south-western sector. Seventh was always smaller, and its work often lonelier, but this numbered air force fielded Liberator bombers through to the end of the war. Furthermore, many of the Navy's PB4Y Liberators and Privateers operated in the same region as Seventh, although not under its command.

The designation of this Hawaii-based headquarters dates to 5 February 1942. Seventh's best-known commander was Maj Gen Willis H Hale, who, it will be recalled, had a role in quashing a rebellion by pilots who wanted B-17s in preference to B-24s. Hale replaced Brig Gen H C Davidson, who in turn had replaced aviation pioneer Maj Gen Clarence L Tinker, lost in an LB-30 in the Battle of Midway. Eventually, Seventh Air Force was to operate in the central and western Pacific areas.

Both the 90th and the 307th BGs were briefly assigned to Seventh en route to their south-western duties in Fifth and Thirteenth Air Forces respectively. VII Bomber Command, as Seventh Air Force's bomber headquarters was known, was left in the early days with only the B-17-

During 18-22 April 1943 two 307th BG squadrons (371st and 372nd) deployed to Funafuti under Seventh Air Force commander Maj Gen Willis Hale to mount a one-time assault on Nauru. Here, Hale's Liberators bomb the atoll on 22 April, ordnance being dropped from a height of 8500 ft (2590 m). Smoke is rising from three bombed-out phosphate plants. The distance from Funafuti to Nauru was 900 miles (1448 km), and although Hale spoke of heavy resistance by Zero fighters, he said that the raid was a success. He added, 'Prior to the war, Japan produced eight per cent of the world's phosphate supply, and no other refineries are now available to the Japs except in the Caroline group' (*via Bill Bartsch*)

Funafuti, where the 307th BG's 371st and 372nd BS (temporarily deployed from Hickam Field, Hawaii) prepare for the 22 April 1943 assault on Nauru. Visible here is a nose turret-equipped B-24D-30-CO (42-40072) flown by a crew headed by a Lt Irby of the 371st BS. A wartime caption tells us that 'because of the small size of the island, adequate dispersal of the Consolidated B-24s was impossible'. Funafuti would not see American bombers on a permanent basis again until November with the arrival of the 42nd BS/11th BG (*via Bill Bartsch*)

equipped 5th BG. By 1943, the 11th BG returned to Hawaii and reconstituted itself as a B-24 Liberator unit, finally giving Seventh the nucleus of a Liberator force. Nevertheless, Seventh was so inadequately equipped that Gen Hale had difficulty meeting an obligation to furnish a daily minimum striking force of 18 heavy bombers. As late as July 1942, Brig Gen Truman H Landon, who reported to Hale as boss of VII Bomber Command, was sceptical that any significant offensive operations could be carried out. Seventh simply did not have enough of anything.

WAKE BATTLE

A remarkable early effort was the 23 December 1942 night attack against Japanese-held Wake Island by 26 B-24Ds of the 307th BG, which dropped 135 500-lb (227-kg) and 21 incendiary bombs. The D-model bombers launched from Hawaii and staged through Midway – an example of the challenge in range and endurance that would confront Liberator crews throughout the war. One of the group's squadrons, the 371st BS, was nicknamed the 'Long Rangers', a name later, and often, applied to the entire group.

After a flurry of battles which gave Liberator crew members eyeball-to-eyeball contact with A6M 'Zeke' and 'Hamp' fighters, and one mishap in which a B-24 collided with a Japanese fighter with the loss of all aboard, Seventh Air Force ended its raids on Wake. They were not to resume until March 1944.

CENTRAL PACIFIC

Pressing the war against Japan in the Ellice, Gilbert, and Marshall Islands, Gen Hale got the green like from Adm Nimitz to bomb Tarawa and Nauru. The job went to the 371st and 372nd BS of the 307th BG, dubbed 'Task Force 12' and under Hale's personal command. Hale reached Funafuti in the Ellice Islands with his B-24 force on 18 April 1943. Funafuti was adequate for bomber operations, but far from lavish with its single 6600-ft (2030-m) runway of crushed coral. Two days later, 22 B-24Ds bombed Nauru. The next day, a dozen Liberators attacked

Tarawa, achieving direct hits on fuel storage and barracks areas. Now, it became time to commit the 11th BG with its inexperienced crews – they came down to Funafuti on 27 June for another raid on Tarawa. What followed was a series of fiascos in which one Liberator crashed on take-off and another soon after, and only two bombers actually reached Tarawa.

As described in the history of the AAF in World War 2, 'Operating thus at extreme range and through the use of an intervening staging point, Seventh Air Force bombers over the long period between the Battle of Midway and the actions preliminary to invasion of the Gilberts had been able to get in an occasional blow at Wake, Tarawa, or Nauru. Such missions (broke) the tedium of routine reconnaissance, but they could have little cumulative effect on the enemy's strength, and serviced chiefly to provide for the crews valuable experience, and for headquarters no less valuable intelligence.'

The official history describes the evolution of the Liberator's warfighting prowess as follows;

'The transition to B-24s for all Pacific heavy bombardment units, begun late in 1942, greatly enhanced the importance of modification as a depot function. The B-24D was sadly lacking in firepower, particularly in the nose of the plane. Japanese pilots soon discovered this defensive weakness with the result that Gen. Landon reported that approximately half of all early enemy fighter attacks on B-24s were made frontally. After Lt Col Marion D Unruh had designed a nose turret to correct the weakness (the turret for which he shares credit with the 90th BG's Col Arthur Rogers), it was installed by the Hawaiian Air Depot in more than 200 B-24s during 1943. B-24 firepower was further improved by the installation of twin

This B-24D-30-CO (42-40089) was one of two Liberators destroyed during a night attack by Japanese bombers on 22 April 1943 in retaliation for the Nauru raid. The location is again Funafuti (*via Bill Bartsch*)

DAISY MAE was a turret-equipped B-24D-15-CO (41-23983) apparently assigned to the 42nd BS/11th BG. The bomber was on a mission from Funafuti to Wake Island on 22 July 1943 when it sustained battle damage, limped away from the battle area, and made a crash landing on Midway. Some crew members were killed and there is conflicting information as to whether the aircraft, which had a crushed port landing gear, ever flew again (*via Bill Bartsch*)

.50-cal (7.62-mm) guns in the belly and tail of the airplane. The depot also moved the navigator's position to the flight deck and developed pilot and co-pilot blister windows to provide greater visibility. It continued to perform these modifications for the Pacific theater until the advent of the B-24J, which included most of the changes.'

DRAB B-24s

Well into mid-1943, all of the Liberators passing through Hawaii and reaching the central Pacific were camouflaged in olive-drab paint with standard US markings. There were still far too few B-24s available as the Allies plotted Operation *Galvanic* – the invasion and occupation of the Gilbert Islands. For *Galvanic*, Seventh had seven squadrons of bombers and three of fighters operating from five islands – Canton, Funafuti, Nukufetau, Nanomea and Baker. The 11th BG's Liberators, launching from Funafuti, did much of the softening up for the Second Marine Division's heroic invasion of Tarawa atoll on 20 November 1943.

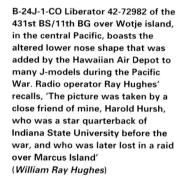

B-24J-1-CO Liberator 42-72982 of the 431st BS/11th BG over Wotje island, in the central Pacific, boasts the altered lower nose shape that was added by the Hawaiian Air Depot to many J-models during the Pacific War. Radio operator Ray Hughes' recalls, 'The picture was taken by a close friend of mine, Harold Hursh, who was a star quarterback of Indiana State University before the war, and who was later lost in a raid over Marcus Island' (*William Ray Hughes*)

Sgt James E Berryhill, a tail gunner of the 431st BS/11th BG, looks back over the twin hand-held .50-cal (12.7-mm) machine-guns of his B-24D Liberator. This photograph illustrates the appearance of the tail gun position on the B-24D and LB-30 Liberator models, which was replaced by a power turret on later Liberators (*Rudy Specter*)

SKY SCOW (42-72987) was the 24th B-24J model manufactured by Consolidated in San Diego, and was piloted by 1Lt John Schellenberger. Here, mechanics repair the bomber, which belongs to the 27th BS/30th BG. It had been damaged in a raid over Jaluit Island in the Marshalls, and was being repaired on Nanumeea, in the Ellice Islands. Note the M4 tracked vehicle behind the wing. The caricature on the nose of this Liberator (the term 'nose art' did not exist during World War 2) appears to show a naked beauty riding a winged helmet. A different aircraft (42-73473) later served in the same squadron as *SKY SCOW III*, but no record has surfaced of a B-24J christened *SKY SCOW II* (*Bill Bartsch*)

A latecomer among Seventh B-24 groups was the 30th BG 'Atoll Busters' (eventually to operate the 27th, 38th, 392nd and 819th BS), which began to assemble in the central Pacific at about the time of the Tarawa landing. The 30th began flying from Nanomea, in the Ellice Islands, on 12 November. Liberators of the 27th BS/30th BG staged through Tarawa on 23 December to escort US Navy photo aircraft over Kwajalein – the largest atoll in the world, soon to be invaded in Operation *Flintlock-Catchpole*. This was the first launch of heavy bombers from the Tarawa atoll, paid for with the blood of Marines.

Typical of grief confronting Liberator crews was a mission flown by *A-VAILABLE* (42-72979), a B-24J-1-CO of the 27th BS/30th BG. This bomber's crew, as one veteran recalls, 'successfully hit Truk Island at night and was caught in heavy AA and searchlights. They dove from 10,000 to 6000 ft (3048 to 8182 m) and performed aerobatic moves to evade Japanese searchlights. Just when they had thought they were free, they were spotted and intercepted by a Zero nightfighter.

'The Zero put five 20-mm cannon shells into the cockpit area, killing the co-pilot and blinding the pilot with flying glass. It also knocked out trim controls, autopilot, greenhouse, interphone, the co-pilot's junction

box and the radio. The waist gunner and top turret finally downed the Zero with a long .50-cal. (12.7-mm) burst. The plane continued to dive, throttle wide open, while other crew members removed the co-pilot's body from the controls.

'Soon after the co-pilot's body was removed the blind pilot recovered the plane from its dive. The plane levelled off at about 3000 ft (914 m). Just when they thought things were improving, the navigator passed out from a leg wound. Now the crew was lost and flying blind in thousands of miles of dark ocean.

'The bombardier sat in the co-pilot's seat and read the instruments that were still functioning to the pilot. They set a heading for the direction they thought Eniwetok was. The pilot, who was about to pass out from his own wounds, managed to continue to fly and give orders to the crew. It was decided that when fuel ran out they would be forced to ditch.

'Orders were given to dump everything that wasn't nailed down overboard. The jackets, guns, ball turret, everything, went over. During the emptying of the aircraft, a 500-lb (227-kg) bomb was found hanging from the rack. They cranked open the bay doors and dislodged the bomb only to have it tangle and hang armed outside the plane. Two men crawled down onto the bay and hoisted it back into the aircraft. As the sun came up, the pilot stated that they would have to ditch. Just as the crew was preparing for a water ditch, an island appeared on the horizon. It was Eniwetok. The bombardier guided the pilot in with verbal commands such as, "Lower, lower" and "a little to the right". The crew braced for a crash landing as A-VAILABLE bounced once and settled in.'

The crew of A-VAILABLE somehow survived, and the bomber was repaired and remained in service until war's end.

Kwajalein was seized in January 1944. According to notes by historian William Bartsch, *Galvanic* and *Flintlock* losses included seven B-24s downed by anti-aircraft fire and nine by Japanese fighters, plus four claimed by operational mishaps and five lost to unknown causes – a total of 25. The 11th BG moved to Kwajalein in April 1944, continuing to attack Japanese installations in the Marshalls and extending its reach into the Caroline and Marianas Islands. As with US air power generally, the mission of the 11th BG was to neutralise Japanese bases so that Navy, Marine and Army forces could leapfrog from point to point without being struck on the flank by Japanese naval and air forces.

AFTER KWAJALEIN

Eniwetok atoll fell to US troops in February 1944. The US advance in the Marshalls now threatened Japanese forces on Truk, in the Carolines – in Japan's view a 'Gibraltar of the Pacific', and a destination Liberator crews were to see all too often. Yet another target was Ponape, in the eastern Carolines. Ponape was struck by 42 B-24s of the 11th and 30th BGs on 15 February 1944.

The effort against Truk was huge and continuous, 22 B-24s staging

42-73029 was a khaki B-24J-5-CO Liberator of the 431st BS/11th BG, the unit being identified by three vertical fin stripes, yellow in colour. This Liberator was photographed flying near Kwajalein, in the Marshall Islands, in June 1944 (*via Allan G Blue*)

through Kwajalein to hit the atoll on 14 March 1944. Twenty-one bombers from the 30th BG returned soon after on a nocturnal mission, and 30 March, Liberators of the 11th BG staged through Eniwetok to attack Truk and Moen Island. In the weeks that followed, Liberators returned to Truk repeatedly. On 3 April Japanese nightfighters appeared at Truk for the first time, blasting two B-24s out of the sky.

As part of an island-hopping strategy aimed at driving relentlessly toward Tokyo, the Pacific commander, Adm Chester Nimitz, in March 1944 ordered US invasion forces to bypass Truk and the rest of the Carolines and drive into the Marianas Islands in Operation *Forager*. The key target became the island of Saipan, where Marines went ashore on Red Beach One on 15 June 1944. Within two weeks landings on Tinian and Guam followed. If the attacks in the Marianas succeeded, the Allies would have bases within striking range of the Japanese home islands for the newest AAF bomber, the B-29 Superfortress. But the road was paved by Liberators.

TRUK AGAIN

The 11th BG bombed Truk again and again in the spring and summer of 1944. During one intercept, single-engined Japanese fighters did not make firing runs with their guns but, instead, tried dropping white-hot phosphorus bombs on the Liberators. Three B-24s passed through this unusual high-temperature blitz and, only with violent evasive action, escaped harm. In later years, veterans of this action would refer to this engagement as one of the first uses of air-to-air missiles, although the phosphorus bombs were actually unguided projectiles.

In August a brace of 11th BG Liberators found themselves being harried by a pair of Kawasaki Ki-45 'Nick' twin-engined fighters. A crew member looked out to see the fighters apparently flying formation beside his bomber. Thereafter, came an air-to-air scuffle that seemed amateurish on the part of the Japanese. A B-24 gunner poured a burst of tracers into

B-24J-1-CO 42-72969 *Our Baby* of the 27th BS/30th BG, piloted by Lt Frederick F Garrett, is seen just prior to being refuelled at Nanumea, in the Ellice Islands, in preparation for a raid on Maleoelap Island, in the Marshalls, on 15 December 1943. This proved to be the bomber's last mission, for it was hit over Taroa and crashed in the sea with the loss of all on board, including the deputy commander of the 30th BG (*via Bill Bartsch*)

1Lt John J 'Jack' Gartland briefs the crew of *GLENNA BEE II*, B-24J-1-CO Liberator 42-73010 of the 98th BS/11th BG on Nukufateau, in the Ellice Islands, which Americans called 'Nookeyfortoo'. *GLENNA BEE II*'s crew was normally headed by 1Lt Thomas M Esmond. This bomber was subsequently transferred to the 26th BS (*via Bill Bartsch*)

Maj Earl J Cooper, commander of the 42nd BS/11th BG, sits astride the radio mast of *PEGGY*, turret-equipped B-24D-20-CO Liberator 41-24110 at Funafuti, in the Ellice Islands, in 1943. Japanese bombers raided Funafuti on the night of 13 November 1943 and destroyed *PEGGY*, which was the sole Liberator lost that night. Incredibly, during the next Japanese air raid four nights later, B-24 42-40688 *WICKED WITCH* became the sole casualty, being destroyed in the same revetment! (*via Bill Bartsch*)

one of the Ki-45s when it attempted an intercept from slightly above and ahead of the bomber. The Japanese aircraft began showering pieces of itself and limped away, rated as a 'probable' kill. The second 'Nick' abruptly became more persistent, making a total of six passes, but they were ineffectual. The bomber crews wondered why the Japanese, whom they respected, did not do better.

Soon afterward, the group was preoccupied with a 28 August 1944 mission to Truk where a furious battle ensued with Zeroes flown by pilots who left no doubt as to their competence.

B-24J-1-CO 42-72992 *COCONUT QUEEN* of the 98th BS/11th BG

was hit by a 20 mm shell which blew out the nose wheel tyre and severed heater, electric and hydraulic lines. The damage was worse than it looked, and would later be cited as strong evidence of the Liberator's ability to take a licking. Pilot, Maj R H Benesch, coaxed the bomber to the staging base at Eniwetok, intending to make a regular wheel landing whilst holding the nose gear off as long as possible. But the gear could not be lowered, so the pilot came in wheels-up. The aircraft travelled 600 ft (965 m) down the centre of the runway in a belly landing so pristine and so devoid of

41

clutter that the bomber was quickly ready to fly again.

THE 494th BG

The AAF's 494th BG 'Kelly's Cobras' (864th, 865th, 866th and 867th BS) was the final Liberator group formed in World War 2. The 494th BG became part of Seventh Air Force as the Marianas campaign (itself, later to be viewed as an island-hopping effort aimed at getting bombers closer to Japan) gathered steam with the invasion of the Palau Islands and Ulithi and Yap, in the Carolines, in mid-September

Hit by anti-aircraft fire during a strike on Jaluit, Lt Kurz's B-24J-5-CO (42-73022) of the 98th BS/11th BG – which never had a nickname – almost returned safely to Nukufateu on 23 November 1943. Hydraulic lines were shot out and there was a large hole in the wing under the no 1 engine. Unable to stop after touching down, the Liberator went off the south end of the runway and ended up some 150 ft (45 m) into the ocean, right-side up, in about four feet (one metre) of water. The aircraft was a total loss, but no one was seriously injured (*via Bill Barstch*)

1944. The 494th BG may have been the first combat group never to have an olive drab Liberator, for when it went into action from Angaur, its J-model 'Libs' were exclusively natural metal, with each squadron adopting a distinctive black marking on the tails of their aircraft – the 864th BS had an arrowhead, the 865th BS a backslash, the 866th BS twin vertical stripes and the 867th BS offset quartered black squares.

Typically, Liberator crews lived in tents and struggled with the elements. Recalling the 494th BG's first base at Anguar, in the Palau Islands, radio operator and top turret gunner Don Davis remembered that, 'There was not much of anything there, just a runway running along the water'. He remembered that the Seventh Air Force was pulling frequent 'hit and run raids' against 'just about every Japanese-held island that was nearby'. This may have been the first war in which conditions improved as the troops went forward, and later, when 'Kelly's Cobras' moved to the Philippines and then to Okinawa, amenities improved.

On 27 October 1944, led by the easygoing but determined Col Laurence Kelly, the 'Cobras' of the 494th BG launched from Anguar to assault nearby Koror, and Yap in the Carolines. They returned in a driving squall singularly or in groups of two and three after challenging, heavy, flak, but no Japanese fighters.

In the G-2 section (Intelligence), photo interpreters looked over aerial shots of a building on Koror surrounded by activity, and decided that it was the Japanese high command in the Palau chain. Maj Duncan McKinnon duly went over the building in his shiny new J-model Liberator and put a 500-lb (227-kg) bomb through its roof. Later, the men of 'Kelly's Cobras' learned that instead of exterminating the Japanese top brass, they had smashed the biggest bordello in the Palau Islands.

The invasion of Leyte on 20 October 1944 and the landings on Luzon on 9 January 1945 marked the Philippine phase of the war for Liberator crews. The 494th BG flew numerous missions to Manila Bay.

In late 1944, the 11th BG moved to Guam to join the Saipan-based 30th BG in pounding Japanese targets in the Marianas. The 30th BG 'Atoll Busters'' travels had proceeded from Nanomea to Abemama on 4 January 1944, to Kwajalein on 20 March 1944 and to Saipan on 4 August 1944. The 30th had already bombed Iwo Jima a couple of times and was

Apparently taken on 6 November 1943, this glimpse of the tropics shows a Liberator arriving at Funafuti, from which the Seventh Air Force waged a prolonged and ferocious campaign. The 42nd BS/11th BG began operations from the airfield later that month, returning to the island from which a temporary deployment had been made the previous April by the 371st and 372nd BS (307th BG) when they bombed Nauru (*via Bill Bartsch*)

Nanumea on 14 December 1943. The 27th and 28th BS (30th BG) were assigned here from the end of 1943 onwards, but the bomber seen behind this baseball game appears to be a Navy PB4Y-1 Liberator (*via Bill Bartsch*)

also attacking Chichi Jima and other Japanese-held islands in the Volcano and Bonin chains. In October, the 11th BG joined the 30th BG in this campaign, which went ahead until Iwo Jima was taken in February 1945.

SOUTH PACIFIC

In July 1942 the AAF agreed to turn over a batch of B-24 Liberators to the US Navy, which designated them PB4Y-1s. The first of these saw combat with Marine reconnaissance squadron VMD-254 which was sent to Espiritu Santo in October 1942. Ultimately, VMD-254 completed 300 photo-reconnaissance sorties from Espiritu Santo and Guadalcanal before it returned to the United States at the start of 1944.

Other Marine photo-recce units which saw action with the PB4Y-1 were VMD-154, beginning in January 1943, and VMD-354 a year later. Marine PB4Y-1 Liberators also served with air groups MAG -14, -15 and -35.

The Navy's baptism of fire in the Liberator came on 13 February 1943 when Bombing Squadron 101 (VB-101) under Cdr Bill Moffett Jr, attacked a brace of Japanese ships between New Guinea and Bougainville in PB4Y-1 Liberators. VB-101 appears to be the only naval squadron to have gone into combat with what were standard glass-nosed B-24D Liberators lacking nose turrets.

VB-102 arrived the following month. The squadron, with Cdr Bruce Van Voorhis as skipper, flew PB4Y-1 Liberators with nose turrets from hot, bleak Henderson Field, Guadalcanal. Van Voorhis was lost trying to

Seen over Truk with ack-ack exploding all around, *KANSAS CYCLONE* was a B-24J-5-CO (42-73025) of the 26th BS/11th BG. On 23 December 1943, the *CYCLONE* took off to bomb Wotje. Obstructed by bad weather, the pilot decided to hit Taroa in the Maloelap atoll. Pounced on by 30 to 40 Zeros, the *CYCLONE, GALVANIZED GOOSE* and *THE DIRTY WOMAN* pressed on into flak over the target, taking hits, then rejoined the battle with the fighters. The *CYCLONE*'s gunners were credited with no fewer than five Zero victories, but the bomber was riddled and one crewman killed. The hydraulics were shot out, one engine was gone and the emergency life raft had been hit and ballooned out and broke free, crippling the rudder as it slipped back into the airstream. However, the pilot successfully landed *KANSAS CYCLONE* at Funafuti seven hours later after a marathon struggle (*AAF*)

sink a seaplane tender off Kapingamarangi, a tiny atoll north-west of the Solomons. For this, he was awarded the Medal of Honor, but a measure of payback was achieved days later when another PB4Y-1 claimed six Zero fighters in a single engagement.

Next came VB-103, which sustained the Navy's first Liberator loss on 24 June 1943 when BuNo 32046 was lost in action.

Navy photo-reconnaissance Liberator squadrons followed. In all, the Navy converted 65 Liberators for photo duty and established four squadrons – VD-1 (January 1943), VD-3 (February 1943), VD-4 (August 1943) and VD-5 (July 1944). The first squadron was formed at Guadalcanal, and Liberator operations commenced in the central Pacific when a PB4Y-1P of VD-3 became the first Allied aeroplane to land on Tarawa – that cluster of atolls won at such terrible price with the blood of the Second Marine Division.

VB-115 joined the war early in 1944 and soon afterward came the Navy's final Liberator squadron, VB-200. At Eniwetok, in the central Pacific, VB-116 began ECM (electronic counter-measures) missions in March 1944, flying PB4Y-1 Liberators modified with installation of the AN/ARC-1 radar intercept receiver – similar to the US Army's SCR-587. The squadron flew three-ship sorties against Japanese radars on Truk, radar maps created as a result of these missions helping carrier aircraft to strike targets there.

B-24 Liberator crew members at Funafuti are briefed for their next mission (*via Bill Bartsch*)

Also at Eniwetok, VB-109 under Cdr 'Bus' Miller wreaked havoc with its PB4Y-1 Privateers, including Miller's *THUNDER MUG* (BuNo 32108). On 4 April 1944 Miller made the first solo attack on the celebrated Japanese fortress at Truk, and bombed a destroyer at anchor in the harbour. Miller then launched a one-man war against Puluwat, an atoll 120 miles (193 km) west of Truk. Having razed almost everything on the island except for a lighthouse that sheltered a gun position, Miller attacked the island for the dozenth time.

A three-inch shell from the anti-aircraft gun exploded under the top turret behind Miller's back and depressed its gun barrels. The gunner kept firing, and .50-cal. (12.7-mm) bullets punched through the cockpit ceiling, wounding Miller and co-pilot Bill Bridgeman as their instrument panel disintegrated and muzzle blast singed their hair. Bleeding from dozens of small wounds, Miller flew the PB4Y 850 miles (1367 km) home to Eniwetok.

GIs in the Ellice Islands load up B-24 Liberators for bombing missions (*via Bill Bartsch*)

VB-104 'Buccaneers' relieved VB-101 in August 1943 amid the alternating mud and dust – mixed with the odour of decomposing bodies – at Guadalcanal. The 'Buccaneers' used their big, four-engined bombers in air-to-air action on numerous occasions, and at least seven pilots shot down Mitsubishi G4M 'Betty' bombers – Lt John Humphrey bagged two in one day.

NAVY MEMORIES

Jim Harvill remembered being 'in the Navy during the war and (flying) in the PB4Y-1 between 1943-45 – starting from the Ellice Islands just prior to the Tarawa (Gilberts) campaign and ending at Okinawa when the war was over.

'The Navy did move onto the later models of B-24s and where up to the J- and K-models. But the planes always had a nose turret called the Erco turret (Electric Resource Co). It was different in that it operated the same way the lower ball turret did – that is the entire turret moved as a single unit. Most other turrets moved as a unit in azimuth, but the sight and guns only moved in elevation and the gunner tilted his head to track the sight. Sometime in early 1944 the ball turret was dropped and the space was used for electronic gear, although the unit was raised and lowered the same way as the old turret.

'The Navy was using the planes primarily for patrol and secondarily for bombing. In early 1944 a Lt Stickle from our squadron initiated the idea of coming into the target area at on-the-surface heights. We would fly in on manual the last 200 miles (322 km/h) at top speed at heights of about 50 ft (15 m). A rather exciting ride. But it worked. We came in several times and the atoll AA crews were still uncovering their guns. Radar then was line of sight only, and antennas never seemed to be over 50 ft (15 m) on the atolls.

'Between campaigns (Gilberts, Marshalls, Marianas, etc) we would usually be doing patrol work, looking for stray cargo ships and any naval forces. When cargo ships were spotted in the atolls, we would start mining the entries to the atoll to force the ships to remain while the harbour was swept to remove the mines. This would give the Fleet time to come in and sink as many ships as possible. We did this several times ourselves. Again, the approach altitude would be as close to the surface as possible. We mined many harbours and soon we noticed the pattern of using fuses on the mines at ports that were bypassed, such as Truk, and duds or even water-filled bombs were used on ports which we later took. The drop time

Seen on 14 December 1943 at Nanumea, in the Ellice Islands, B-24J-1-CO Liberator 42-72966, piloted by 1Lt Francis Stafford of the 38th BS/30th BG, Seventh Air Force, displays a painting and the sort of nickname that adorned many bombers. Curiously, the term 'nose art' apparently did not exist during World War 2 – crews spoke only of pictures, or caricatures, or cartoons or paintings – but the work of many skilled artists created pictures like this that leave us with a lasting memory (*via Bill Bartsch*)

B-24J-20-CO Liberator 42-109951 *MADAME PELE* was named after the Hawaiian goddess of fire. Here, it is seen leading another 11th BG B-24 away from a mid-1944 attack on Truk. The target is Dublon Island, while at the lower right is Eten Island, home of a cratered airfield. In the background, hidden by cloud, is Moen Island (*via Bill Bartsch*)

for mines would be right at dusk, light enough to get oriented for the atoll entrances and soon dark enough to make it difficult to spot the mine size and drop locations. They had no choice but to sweep all mined harbours or ignore them. There were too many harbours mined with the real think to make it hard for them to ignore the mining. The mines had delay washers which delayed the time the mine would be armed (up to four days), and counters that could be selected from one to ten for the number of times the mine could be swept before blowing up.

'We also did escort for the photo-planes that came up from the Solomons to photograph the soon-to-be invaded islands. These flight were done at about 22,000 ft (6705 m). The Zeroes would come up in swarms and hassle us. The photo-planes (also B-24s) would be flying a straight line across the atoll and back. I think most of this work was stopped in mid-1944 as the squadrons coming out after that did not have any oxygen tanks or electric suits.

'Also in 1944, we saw our first PB4Y-2s (Privateers), and they were designed for low altitude, long-range work only. In 1945 we spent much of our time cruising up and down the China coast looking for ships trying to reach Japan by hugging the coast and making a dash across the sea to the home islands. The same was also being done between Korea and Japan. We had fewer problems with Zeroes then. We would see the *kamikazes* coming down from Japan to attack the fleet, but they would never let us get close enough to them . . .'

The Navy squadrons in the Seventh Air Force area of operations did not report to AAF commanders, even though they sometimes used the same airfields. As for Seventh Air Force, the official combat history tells us only that it 'served in combat in the central and western Pacific'. Following Maj Gen Hale, other wartime commanders were Maj Gen Robert W Douglass Jr (15 April 1944) and Maj Gen Thomas D White (23 June 1945). The official history does not confirm what many veterans remember – that Seventh was made a part of Far East Air Forces, or FEAF (Chapter Five) in the spring of 1945.

Although Seventh Air Force was always numerically a small air force, the achievements of its Liberator squadrons were larger than life.

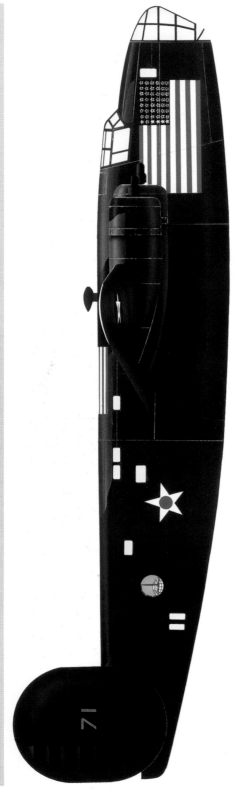

1
B-24A 40-2371 flown by 1Lt Ted Faulkner, 88th Reconnaissance Squadron, Pearl Harbor, 7 December 1941

2
LB-30 AL576 flown by 1Lt William Bayse, 11th BS/7th BG, Java, January 1942

3

LB-30 AL640 *Jungle Queen* of the 397th BS/6th BG, Panama Canal Zone, 1942-43

4

B-24D-15-CO 41-24074 *Tokio Express* of the 319th BS/90th BG at Port Moresby, November 1942

5
B-24D-7-CO 41-23849 *The EAGER BEAVER* flown by 1Lt Charles Whitlock, 320th BS/90th BG, Port Moresby, 1942-43

6
B-24D-65-CO 42-40522 *DELIVERER* flown by 1Lt David T Brennan, 531st BS/380th BG, New Guinea, July 1943

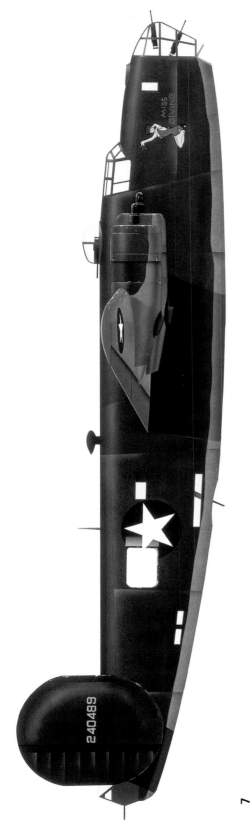

7
B-24D-65-CO 42-40489 *MISS GIVING* flown by 1Lt Jack R Banks, 528th BS/380th BG, Fenton, August 1943

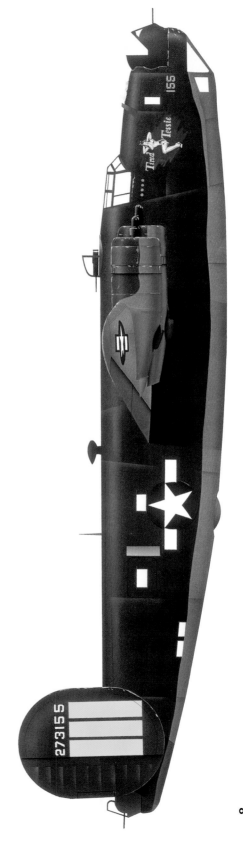

8
B-24J-15-CO 42-73155 *Tired Tessie* flown by 1Lt John Snyder, 431st BS/11th BG, Funafuti, late 1943

9
PB4Y-1 BuNo 32081 *WHITSSHITS* flown by VB-104 XO, Cdr Whit Wright, Guadalcanal, late 1943

10
B-24D-170-CO 42-72963 of the 42nd BS/11th BG, Funafuti, November 1943

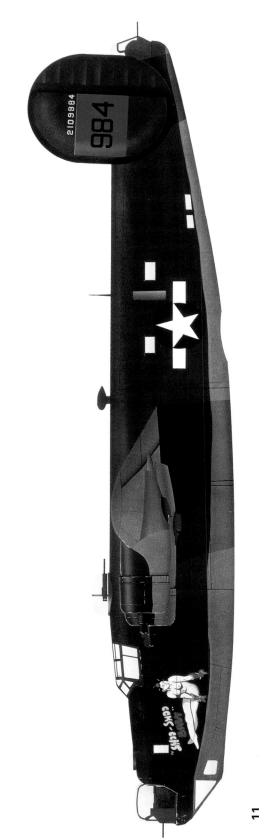

11

B-24J-160-CO 42-109984 "*SHOO-SHOO BABY*" of the 408th BS/22nd BG, Nadzab, February 1944

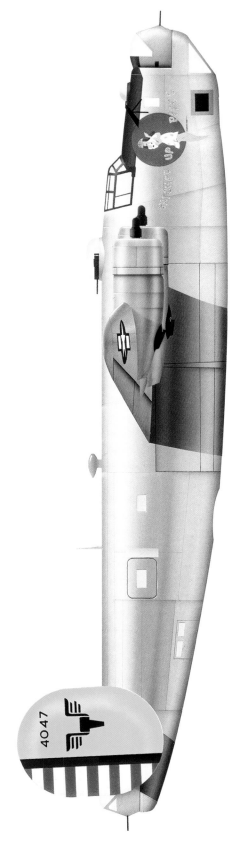

12

F-7A 42-64047 *PATCHED UP PIECE* of the 20th CMS, Morotai, 14 August 1944

13
B-24D-155-CO 42-72783 *Heather Angel* of the 372nd BS/307th BG, Noemfoor, September 1944

14
B-24J-165-CO 44-40532 *NIGHT MISSION* flown by 1Lt Winton E Newcomb, 819th BS/30th BG, Saipan, October 1944

15
SB-24J-85-CO 42-100271 'Snooper' *Lady June* of the 868th BS, Noemfoor, 19 October 1944

16
B-24D -160-CO 42-72815 *"SKY WITCH"* flown by Capt J Ryan, 400th BS/90th BG, Mokmer airstrip, Biak, November 1944

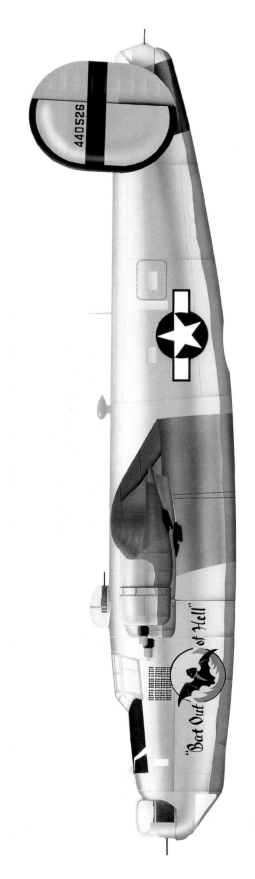

17
B-24J-165-CO 44-40526 *"Bat Out of Hell"* of the 819th BS/30th BG, Saipan, late 1944

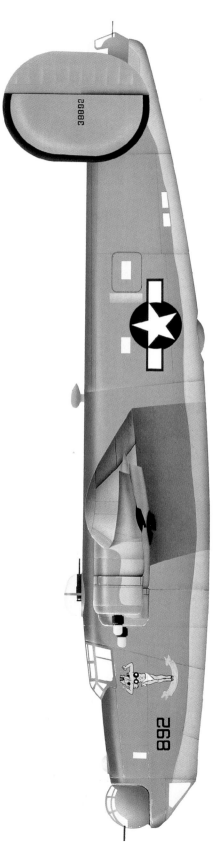

18
PB4Y-1 BuNo 38892 *LADY LUCK* of Lt Cdr J V Barry, VPB-111, late 1944

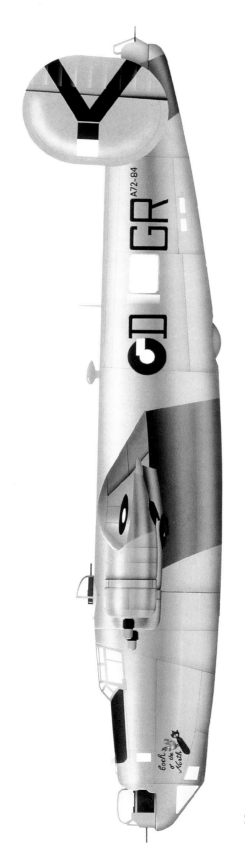

19
B-24L-5-CO A72-84 (formerly 44-41456) *Cock o' the North*, No 24 Sqn, RAAF, Fenton, late 1944

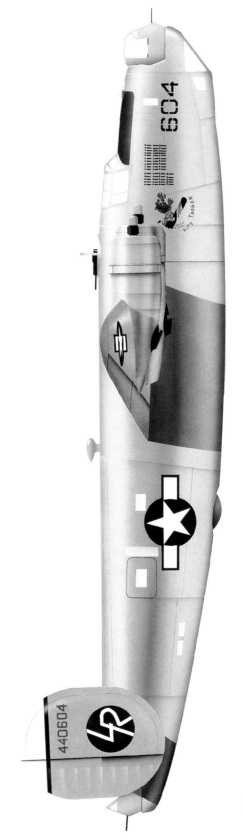

20
B-24J-170-CO 44-40604 *KIT'S TADGER* of the 371st BS/307th BG, McGuire's Field, Mindoro, the Philippines, January 1945

21
B-24J-150-CO 44-40193 *BOOBY TRAP* flown by Squadron Commander, Maj Stanley P Robeck, 321st BS/90th BG, McGuire Field, Mindoro, the Philippines, February 1945

22
B-24J-180-CO 44-40759 *Shack Bunny* of the 867th BS/494th BG, Angaur, March 1945

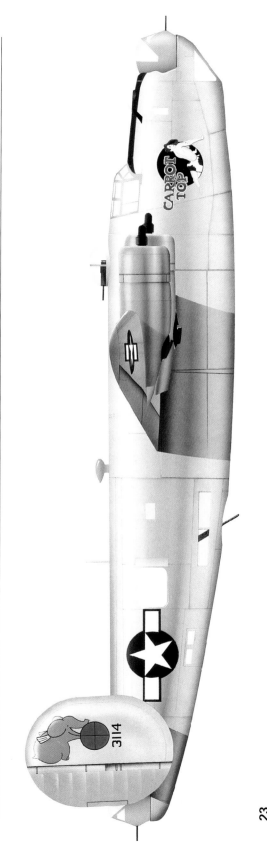

23
B-24J-10-CO 42-73114 *CARROT TOP* of the 528th BS/380th BG, McGuire Field, Mindoro, the Philippines, March 1945

24
B-24M-30-FO 44-51589 of the 29th BS, Galapagos Islands, April 1945

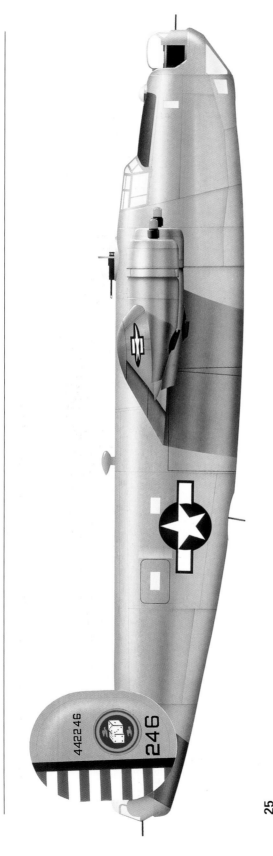

25
B-24M-20-CO 44-42246 of the 65th BS/43rd BG, Clark Field, Luzon, the Philippines, May 1945

26
B-24M-1-CO 44-41809 *"Out Of The Night II"* of the 63rd BS/43rd BG, Clark Field, Luzon, the Philippines, 19 May 1945

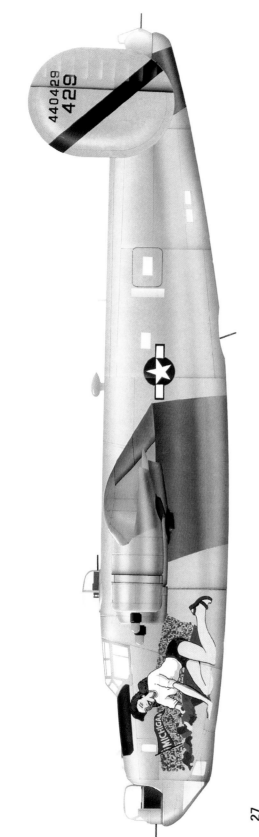

27

B-24J-160-CO 44-40429 *MICHIGAN* of the 64th BS/43rd BG, Clark Field, Luzon, the Philippines, June 1945

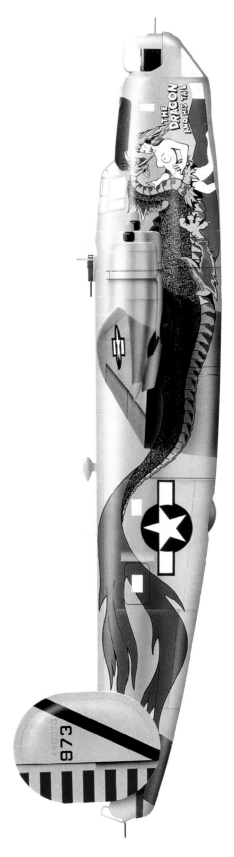

28

B-24J-190-CO 44-40973 *THE DRAGON AND HIS TAIL* of the 64th BS/43rd BG, Ie Shima, mid-1945

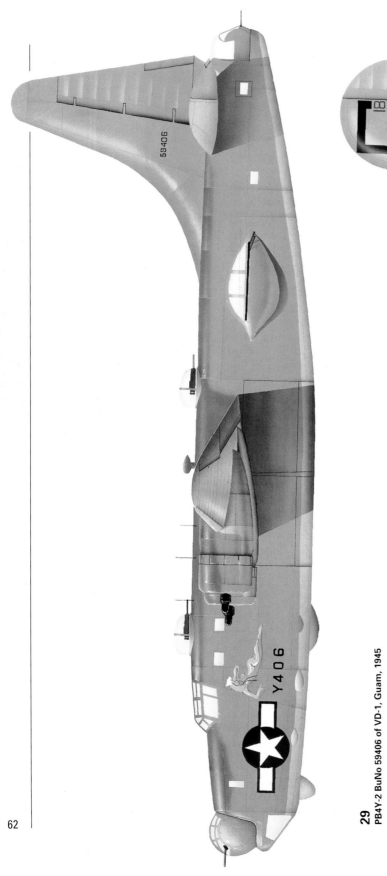

29
PB4Y-2 BuNo 59406 of VD-1, Guam, 1945

30
B-24M-30-CO 44-42418 *"Miss Ileene"* of the 23rd BS/5th BG, Samar, the Philippines, 1945

1
T/Sgt Robert O Spindler, radio
operator with the 64th BS/43rd BG,
Fifth Air Force, at Port Moresby, New
Guinea, in February 1944

2
Maj Austin Straubel, commander
of the 11th BS (Heavy), part of the
7th BG, on Java in January 1942

3
Pilot 1Lt John F Lance of the 23rd
BS/5th BG, Thirteenth Air Force, at
Morotai in November 1944

4
**Gunner S/Sgt William L Adair of the
23rd BS/5th BG, Thirteenth Air Force,
at Morotai in November 1944**

5
**Maj Gen Willis Hale, commander of
the Seventh Air Force**

6
**First lieutenant navigator at
Townsville, in Queensland, Australia,
in 1942**

THIRTEENTH AIR FORCE

T hirteenth Air Force was constituted on 14 December 1942, its first commander being Maj Gen Nathan F Twining, who became one of the premier 'bomber generals' who ran the Air Force in postwar years. After a brief set-up period at Noumea, New Caledonia, Thirteenth moved its headquarters to Espiritu Santo, where it remained for a year. During this time, Allied troops invaded Guadalcanal and became caught up in furious fighting in the air and on the ground.

The 307th BG brought the B-24 Liberator to Thirteenth's area of operations in February 1943. Initially with two squadrons (370th and 424th BS, joined on Guadalcanal in June 1942 by the 371st and 372nd BS), the 307th BG established its base at Carney Field, on Guadalcanal, then moved forward to Henderson Field, where they were joined by Navy PB4Y-1 Liberators of VB-101. Liberators began harrying Japanese shipping near Guadalcanal and Bougainville.

Like most outfits in the Pacific at the time, the 307th BG offered little in the way of distinctive aircraft markings, although early B-24Ds had black undersides – a left-over from a mission to Wake Island in December 1942. Liberators rotated through the Hawaiian air depot, where power turrets were installed in the nose, but they came back to Guadalcanal still without flair or colour. As the war progressed, the 307th BG's bombers began to acquire nicknames and art, although it was not until mid-1944 that the group began to wear a stylised 'LR' (for 'Long Rangers') against a circle of insignia blue on the outer, lower fin of its 'Libs'. By then, of course, the ubiquitous D-models were being replaced by B-24J, L and M variants.

A typical strike was flown on 14 February 1943 when nine PB4Y-1s, assisted by ten P-38 Lightnings and a dozen F4U Corsairs, sought out Japanese vessels near Buin. The Liberators bombed several ships, but were intercepted by Mitsubishi A6M Zeroes and F1M 'Pete' floatplane fighters. A Zero put cannon fire into the cockpit of a PB4Y-1 and sent it plunging into the sea. A second Liberator sustained hits from anti-aircraft fire and ditched near New Georgia, although the escort fighters claimed three aerial victories and PB4Y-1 crews staked a

The US Navy's PB4Y-1 Liberator began combat operations in the Pacific in 1943. Most, but not all, Navy Liberators differed from AAF bombers in having a bulbous Erco 250 SH ball turret with two .50-cal (12.7-mm) guns, as seen here, fitted in the nose. Side number B82 (BuNo 65299, or B-24L-15-CO 44-41715) strikes a classic pose for a Navy Liberator, replete with a yagi antenna on the lower fuselage below the pilot and guns protruding in all directions. This aircraft served with VD-1 (*via Ronald R Sathre*)

claim for no fewer than nine Zeroes! Japanese records report the loss of just three aircraft that day.

THE 5th BG

The 'Bomber Barons' of the 5th BG (23rd and 31st BS) were the next Liberator outfit in the Thirteenth Air Force combat zone. The 5th BG's war was to become a litany of geographic names little-known

Khaki B-24J-30-CO 42-73271 of the 371st BS/307th BG 'Long Rangers' is seen on a combat mission from Carney Field, on Guadalcanal, apparently in October 1943 (*Roderick Smith/Pima Air and Space Museum*)

before the war and not long remembered after – the 'Barons' flew from Guadalcanal (19 August 1943), Munda, New Georgia (4 February 1944), Momote, Los Negros (7 April 1944) and (after the formation of Far East Air Forces, covered in the next chapter), Noemfoor (22 September 1944), Morotai (October 1944) and Samar, in the Philippines (5 March 1945).

Formerly equipped with B-17E/F Flying Fortresses, the 'Bomber Barons' did not at first have distinctive markings on their olive-drab B-24Ds. Eventually, however, a blue shield appeared across the outer fins of 5th BS bombers as a group marking, dissected by a diagonal band that acted as the individual squadron colour. As the war progressed, the group quickly obtained natural metal B-24J, L and M model Liberators. A handful of talented artists painted nicknames and caricatures on some of the bombers, but many boasted no such individuality.

Later, when the 5th BG had four squadrons in the field, 'battle numbers' or 'plane in group' numbers were assigned, and geometric symbols appeared above these on the fins as follows: 01 to 25 beneath a square (23rd BS); 26 to 50 beneath a triangle (31st BS); 51 to 75 beneath a circle (72nd BS); and 76 to 99 under a diamond (394th BS).

As they slogged in the same region as the better-known bomber groups of Gen Kenney's Fifth Air Force, some members of the Thirteenth felt a little like orphans, and wondered if anyone knew they were there. Day-to-day operational control of bombing sorties by these AAF Liberators was determined by the naval command. The Pacific Ocean Areas (an official term) under Adm Chester Nimitz included the South Pacific, which was commanded by Adm Ghormley. Originally, the 160th Parallel was the dividing line between the South Pacific and South-west Pacific theatres,

A scene that was repeated too often beneath the palm fronds of the Pacific – a B-24 Liberator in trouble, its landing wheel collapsing on landing after a mission. The 'meat wagon' (4x4 truck converted into an ambulance) is ready (*via Bill Bartsch*)

'War has its beauty', suggested the original caption to this shot of a Liberator passing over palm trees. The location is Makin Island (*via Bill Bartsch*)

although this was moved further west to the 159th Parallel to include Guadalcanal, which was planned to be a Marine operation.

B-24 pilot 1Lt John Lance remembered the contrast between the two numbered air forces;

'The speciality of Thirteenth was long-range unescorted formation missions, and we held all the records for that sort of thing. Our outfit (23rd BS/5th BG) was very different from those in Fifth Air Force. They were called "MacArthur's Airman". This was considered high praise, the public having totally ignored MacArthur's failure on the first day of the war, and for some reason the lens always seemed to focus on the arrogant, aloof, MacArthur, rather than the easygoing, understated, Kenney.

'They always got attention in the newspaper and radio dispatches out of Australia and San Francisco', Lance continued. '"MacArthur's airmen" had the same defence we did, except we had these specially designed planes with belly turrets, which gave more protective power for a group that was flying unescorted'. Lance was referring to the ball turret, which many bomb groups in the Pacific dispensed with. Lance felt it was always difficult to lay on fighter escort because 'we went from a sort of pinpoint in the ocean to another pinpoint and back again after bombing, so the fighters would have to fly all the distance of the mission and use up extra fuel in dogfights over the target . . .'

On 27 July 1943 Brig Gen Ray L Owens replaced Twining as commander of Thirteenth Air Force – Owens had logged considerable time in B-24s. The headquarters for Thirteenth (never, necessarily, the same as the location of its two B-24 groups, the 5th BG and 307th BG) moved from Espiritu Santo to Guadalcanal on 13 January 1944.

THE 868th 'SNOOPERS'

In the early days on Guadalcanal in August 1943, a unique squadron within Thirteenth Air Force was the predecessor of the 868th BS (Heavy), which operated autonomously – it was often co-located with the 5th BG, but was not subordinate to the group – and which used Liberators equipped with airborne radar for low-level attacks at night and pathfinder operations. The 868th 'Snoopers' covered vast distances from the south-west Pacific to the doorstep of Japan, operating from Munda (1 January 1944), Los Negros (20 January 1944), Noemfoor (29 August 1944), Morotai (22 March 1945), Leyte (3 July 1945) and Okinawa (29 July 1945). One man, armament officer Capt Robert H Shively, had

the distinction of serving in the 'Snoopers' from their formation on Munda until VJ-Day.

The 'Snoopers' began as a cadre of skilled personnel from the 394th BS/5th BG (with a few from the 307th BG). Their radar equipment and techniques came from the confusingly-named 'Colonel Wright's Project' located at Langley Field, Virginia, and their radar-equipped Liberators were usually known as SB-24s. They were equipped with SRC-717-B search and navigation radar, AN/APQ-5 LABS bombing radar, SCR-729 IFF (identification, friend or foe) and an AN/ARN-1 radio altimeter. The antenna for the SC-717-B was placed in the bomber's ball turret location.

Initially operating as the 394th BS/5th BG, the 'Snoopers' flew from Guadalcanal and attacked Japanese shipping between Rabaul and the Solomons. They arrived on Munda at the end of 1943, and by the time the unit acquired the 868th BS designation, it had already been credited with the sinking of 34,000 tons of enemy shipping.

One particular action involving the 868th BS caught the attention of Thirteenth Air Force boss, Gen George C Kenney, who wrote following report;

'On the night of 16 October 1944), Maj Weston, the operations officer of the 868th (BS), left his desk to do his share of the squadron's work and took off on a shipping search of the Macassar Straits, with his secondary target the Lutong oil facilities. Not finding anything on his shipping search, he arrived at Lutong at day-break. Weston said everything seemed peaceful and quiet, so he took his

Close-up of the refuelling of a turret-equipped, khaki-camouflaged B-24D Liberator on a Pacific island (*via Bill Bartsch*)

B-24D-50-CO 42-40323 *Frenisi* (named, replete with spelling error, for the popular song 'Frenesi') completed 100 combat missions with the 370th BS/307th BG and was scheduled for a war bond tour that never materialised. A wartime caption tells us that this is *Frenisi* returning from sortie number 100, but this is almost certainly a re-enactment for publicity cameras that took place in July 1944 (*via Allan G Blue*)

Frenisi, equipped with a Consair A-6 nose turret installed in Hawaii, is seen here re-enacting her return from her 100th combat mission for the press camera in early July 1944. This bomber never wore the 307th BG's 'LR' symbol on the fin, but the words *THE LONG RANGERS* were added in an arc beneath the serial number (*via Allan G Blue*)

42-110147 was a khaki B-24J-30-CO Liberator of the 370th BS/307th BG, seen here in July 1944 (*Pima Air and Space Museum*)

B-24 down on the deck and flew between two rows of big 50,000-barrel oil tanks. The boys firing out the waist window on the right side set fire to four tanks and the gunners firing out the waist windows on the left got seven tanks. Weston then did a 180-degree turn and came back between two rows of barracks, and gave them the same treatment as the oil tanks, while the Japanese were firing out the windows with small-calibre rifles. There were no casualties on the crew, but 164 bullet holes were counted in the B-24 when it landed.

'That crew had accomplished in 20 minutes a job that I would have considered excellent for a whole group of bombers if I had sent them out for the special purpose of destroying the oil storage at Lutong. We had no way of knowing how full the tanks were at the time they were burned and destroyed, but the Nip had lost at least a half million barrels of storage capacity . . .'

Kenney had a special interest in the 868th BS because his son, Bill, was a member.

Throughout the early and middle months of 1943, Liberators flew long-distance missions with small numbers of aircraft. On 18 June 1943 the 307th BG flew a 1700-mile (2735 km) round-trip to bomb Nauru. The bombers arrived as the sun came up, and their bombs touched off large fires. US forces began the process of taking New Georgia in late June. While fighting near the airfield at Munda persisted in July, the 'Long Rangers' bombed airfields at Kahili and Buka. These targets, together with Buin, were hit repeatedly not only by Liberators,

69

B-24J Liberators of the 424th BS/307th BG attack Koror, in the Palau Islands, on 2 September 1944 (*via Allan G Blue*)

B-24D-35-CO 42-40212 *SHADY LADY* of the 370th BS/307th BG in December 1944. One of the few D-models to have a Consair A-6 nose turret grafted onto its nose, as seen here, and subsequently replaced by the traditional glass nose, this bomber was later used for 'hack' duties at Hickam Field, Hawaii. This photo in the battle zone was taken in about December 1944 (*Roderick Smith/Pima Air and Space Museum*)

but by SBD Dauntlesses and TBF Avengers that took on shipping just offshore. On 25 July 1943, Liberators joined with SBDs and TBFs to fly a mission supporting troops on the ground. After a bitter fight, US troops seized Munda – future home of many Liberators – on 5 August.

Thereafter, Thirteenth Air Force's bomb groups rotated between the forward area and the rear, except when a significant mission required all to participate. The 5th BG's 23rd and 72nd BS got a chance to rest in August 1943, while the 31st BS took over the group's commitment on Guadalcanal. The other groups rotated squadrons similarly.

Kahili was a recurring target. One night when Liberators were returning to Guadalcanal from that busy Japanese airfield, two G4M1 'Betty' bombers slid into their formation, running lights on. One used this ploy to get close to the transport ship *John Penn*, which it proceeded to sink with a torpedo. The anti-aircraft fire which ensued was meant for the Japanese bombers, but the Liberator of 5th BG commander, Lt Col Marion D Unruh, took substantial hits. Unruh landed the bomber at Carney Field with one landing wheel jammed in the up position and one down.

Liberators flew day and night missions to support the Allied effort to take Bougainville in late 1943. 'One day when they were coming up at us, I saw a beautiful sight', remembered S/Sgt Frederic Neumann, a waist gunner with the 394th BS/5th BG – which had surrendered its 'Snooper' mission to the 868th BS, and was now flying conventional high-altitude strikes. 'I saw this Japanese twin-engined fighter flying in a lazy arc, kind of getting into position for a run on us, when it collided with a Japanese single-engine fighter. It shouldn't have been possible to hear anything from that distance, because we were maybe a quarter of a mile away, but I swear I heard this loud, rending sound and there were pieces of metal spraying all around like flakes of pepper. Several of us observed this, and we did not see any parachutes."

One of the favourite targets on Kahili was the fighter base. On 10 October 1943 it was struck by Liberators of the 'Bomber Barons'' 72nd BS. Despite P-38 Lightnings being in the air to contend with a 'greeting' by 15 Zeroes, the Japanese fighters managed to shoot down one bomber. A gunner aboard a B-24 was credited with one of the Mitsubishi fighters destroyed in return. More raids followed, including one on 15 October 1943 when Corsairs and Lightnings protected Liberators over Kahili. Attacks on this and other airfields continued through October, with Liberators being joined repeatedly by TBF Avengers, SBD Dauntlesses and PV-2 Venturas.

Marines established a beachhead on Bougainville on 1 November 1943. Some of the Japanese bases in the region became ineffectual as the advance continued, but Rabaul was always posed a problem – it was often the source of Japanese warships and aircraft that confounded the Allies at every turn – and Liberators went to visit frequently. Indeed, during one of the early raids a 'Snooper' SB-24 apparently disabled the Japanese heavy cruiser *Haguro*, which was the flagship of the Emperor's formidable forces.

T/Sgt Harry L Walker, a flight engineer and top turret gunner with the 370th BS/307th BG, cleans his guns at Morotai in December 1944 (*Pima Air and Space Museum*)

"Munda Belle" was a black-bellied SB-24D-CO (42-40144) 'Snooper' that served with the 370th BS/307th BG before being transferred to the special-mission 868th BS. The 'last four' of the serial number of this D-model are repeated in different sizes on the nose. This portrait was snapped at the Thirteenth Air Force depot in New Caledonia (*via William Hess*)

Thirteenth Air Force bombers mounted a major effort against Rabaul on 11 November 1943, the initial wave consisting of two-dozen Fifth Air Force Liberators sent to bomb Lakunai airfield. Naval aeroplanes from no fewer than five aircraft carriers also struck in, and around, Rabaul before a giant force – by Pacific standards at least – of 42 Liberators from the 5th and 307th BGs arrived on the scene. The 'Bomber Barons' and 'Long Rangers' staged through Munda, and most of them bombed through the clouds from heights as great as 23,000 ft (7010 m). Four fighters were also claimed by Liberator gunners.

B-24J-170-CO Liberator 44-40604 *KIT'S TADGER* of the 371st BS/307th BG 'Long Rangers' was hit in the ball turret by Japanese gunfire during a 24 January 1945 mission to bomb the seaplane base at Canacao, near Cavite in Manila Bay. The gunner's body was suspended in the debris until it fell away into the sea, and both waist gunners and a photographer were also seriously wounded. The aircraft recovered at an advanced base in San Jose, Mindoro, in the Philippines (*Pima Air and Space Museum*)

RABAUL SIEGE

In November and December Thirteenth Air Force Liberators virtually wiped out remaining Japanese resistance on Bougainville with repeated bombing raids at all altitudes. The ex-394th BS SB-24 'Snoopers' (previously described) arrived at Munda on 28 December 1943 and acquired their 868th BS designation when the new year. They claimed responsibility in 1943 for the destruction of 34,000 tons of Japanese shipping, including a carrier, two destroyers and two submarines, although Japanese records seem not to confirm any of the vessel losses.

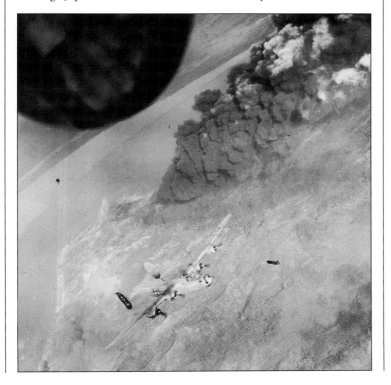

The 5th Bombardment Group (Heavy), Thirteenth Air Force, returns to Balikpapan. The Japanese refinery complex on Borneo was one of the 'most bombed' targets of the war, being struck intermittently from 1942 through to 1945. This is one of several attacks that took place late in the war after Balikpapan no longer inspired the apprehension it might have evoked at an earlier time (*via Allan G Blue*)

A 23rd BS/5th BG Liberator pulls away from a burning refinery at Balikpapan, which once provided seven million barrels of high-octane gasoline annually to the Japanese war machine. Balikpapan was first visited by 11th BS/7th BG LB-30 bombers during the losing battle on Java in early 1942, and remained a high priority to the Allies throughout the war (*via Allan G Blue*)

It is dusk in the Pacific and the distinctive shape of the Erco nose turret tells us that this is a PB4Y-1 Liberator. Unfortunately, when Vice Adm John T 'Chick' Hayward donated this image to the US Navy's pictorial files, he left no date or location (*USN*)

The siege of Rabaul continued, with Liberators participating along with other aeroplanes on raids staged on 19, 23 and 24 December. On Christmas day a handful of Liberators of the 5th BG got through brooding weather to bomb Lakunai. Persistent raids continued through the remainder of the year, but a painful loss was suffered when the Liberator flown by Col Marion D Unruh went down. Although search aircraft located the 'Bomber Barons'' group commander and seven other crew members the next day, and dropped supplies to them, none of the men was ever seen again. One of the true leaders in the Liberator's war against Japan (and a pioneer on B-24D nose turrets) was gone – command of the 5th BG passed to Lt Col Joseph E Reddoch Jr.

Again and again Rabaul was pounded. On 22 January 1944 33 Liberators and half a dozen B-25 Mitchells journeyed to the Japanese bastion. Four days later, Liberators struck Lakunai again. By the end of January no fewer than eight Liberators had been lost over Rabaul and the airfield. Altogether, in the first three months of 1944, Thirteenth Air Force dropped 4632 tons of bombs on Rabaul.

In the spring of 1944, attention shifted to Truk, in the Carolines, and Liberators of Thirteenth Air Force squadrons became frequent visitors.

Thirteenth Air Force headquarters moved from Hollandia, New Guinea, on 13 September 1944 and to Noemfoor ten days later. Even after the creation of FEAF, Thirteenth maintained its separate identity, with its headquarters moving to Morotai on 29 October 1944 and to Leyte on 1 March 1945.

KENNEY SUMMIT

In January 1944 Gen Kenney flew to Washington for a conference with AAF boss Gen Henry H 'Hap'

Pranged-up PB4Y-1 Liberator BuNo 31939 (B-24D-7-CO 41-23829, the fourth Liberator acquired by the Navy) of VB-108 is seen at O'Hare Field, Apamama, Gilbert Islands, on 5 January 1944 (*via Jim Sullivan*)

Arnold. As usual, Kenney asked for reinforcements and more aeroplanes. He was told that everything was going to Europe, but there was a plan that would increase his strength. At that time the South Pacific command was winding up its campaign in the Admiralties and it would no longer have a combat mission since the Pacific War was now moving further north into the central Pacific and northward out of New Guinea. According to Kenney, Thirteenth Air Force would no longer be needed in the south-west Pacific, which was becoming a supply base, and he therefore proposed to Arnold that it be turned over to him. Gen Kenney returned to Australia on the same aeroplane as Maj Gen Hubert R 'Miff' Harmon, who later became Thirteenth commander on 7 January 1944.

While Arnold and Army chief of staff Gen George C Marshall knew that the south-west Pacific presence would be folding, they had not yet decided what to do with Thirteenth Air Force. They liked Kenney's idea and recommended it to the Joint Chiefs. Arnold was already planning to bring home Thirteenth commander Maj Gen Harmon, and he told Kenney he would send Maj Gen St Clair Streett to take command of Thirteenth. Streett took the helm at Thirteenth on 15 June 1944 – the day the Far East Air Forces (FEAF) was organised, with Kenney in command. As noted in Chapter Two, Maj Gen Ennis Whitehead took command of Fifth Air Force, and the numbered air forces continued their distinct identities while serving as part of FEAF. The formation of FEAF was comparable to the arrangement reached half a world away when Eighth and Fifteenth Air Forces were placed under the control of the Strategic Air Forces, Europe.

B-24J-165-CO (44-40467) of the 5th BG on a Pacific mission in 1944 (*via Allan G Blue*)

FAR EAST AIR FORCES

The industrial complex and oil refinery centre at Balikpapan, on Borneo, was a target for American bombers from those earliest days on Java until very late in the war – with a huge gap in between. It was Japan's second biggest source of refined petroleum, behind Palembang on Sumatra, and after raids in 1943, Gen Kenney had noted that Japanese fighter units were short on fuel for a time.

By the time the Thirteenth Air Force turned serious attention to Balikpapan at the end of September 1944, the war was turning against the Japanese, and Thirteenth had become part of the combined Far East Air Forces (FEAF), headed by Kenney.

1Lt John F Lance of the 23rd BS/5th BG 'Bomber Barons' remembered that while the enemy still held the Philippines, the Americans were moving across the South-west Pacific from the New Hebrides and Guadalcanal. 'We took various land bases that the Japanese had along the New Guinea coast. The little island of Biak off the north end of Geelvink Bay in New Guinea was one of the bloodiest fights that (American troops) had in the south-west Pacific. We took the island of Noemfoor, and my group (5th BG) was stationed there for awhile.'

Lance's memories stand as testimony to the back-breaking flying conditions and hard-fought combat of all Liberator crews in the region. 'The 30 September 1944 raid on Balikpapan was launched from our western arc of bases that the United States had at that time. We were about as far west as you could get and still be in places under our control. The raid was assembled from several different bases, from Noemfoor,

B-24J *"Shack Bunny"* of the 867th BS/494th BG is seen flying over the Gulf of Davao en route to bomb Japanese installations around Mintal airfield, a few miles west of the city of Davao, on the Philippine island of Mindanao. The date is March 1945 (*via William Hess*)

The AAF never purchased the extended-fuselage, single-tail, PB4Y-2 Privateer, but US Navy patrol squadrons flew Privateer sorties against Japan up to the end of the war. BuNo 59402, nicknamed *MODEST O'MISS*, of VPB-118 suffered a mishap apparently during an emergency landing at Motoyama airfield No 1 on Iwo Jima in March 1945 (*via Jim Sullivan*)

which had two groups out of the Thirteenth Air Force, and some other bases out of the Australian command.

'The mission was conceived as being a very important thing for depriving the Japanese of a lot of the fuel, and knocking down their morale some. It was an almost impossible mission, on paper. The round-trip distance was greater than any mission that had been flown up to that time for daylight bombardment. The trouble was it was just so damned far that you couldn't carry a full bomb load. We had the maximum gasoline load you could put into the planes.'

The 372nd/307th BG also participated in the Balikpapan raid from Noemfoor. While Thirteenth bomber units were still staging for the attack, Fifth was stripping excess weight from its B-24s, including armour plate and any remaining ball turrets. The 90th BG 'Jolly Rogers', 5th BG 'Bomber Barons' and 307th BG 'Long Rangers' all launched from Noemfoor just after midnight at the start of 30 September, determined to conserve fuel to the maximum for a long trip that would place them in a sky full of flak and fighters. All involved in this strike on Balikpapan believed it was the longest mission ever flown by B-24s.

The 5th BG 'Bomber Barons'' original unit marking comprised a blue shield containing a diagonal stripe, which was applied on the fins of its Liberators. In May 1945, however, the 23rd BS/5th BG began employing a black square that enclosed the radio call number ('tail number') on the fin. In the lead at the lower left is B-24M-20-CO 44-42245 *TOP O'THE MARK* – the name of the penthouse night spot at the Mark Hopkins Hotel in San Francisco. Beneath these bombers is the Allied invasion fleet approaching the coast of Borneo (*via Allan G Blue*)

It was broad daylight, some nine hours and 1243 miles (2000 km) from take-off, when 23 Liberators of the 5th BG made it to the rendezvous point and assaulted Balikpapan. Two Japanese fighters picked them up 250 miles (400 km) out and accompanied them to the target, where a further thirty awaited their arrival. Five minutes behind them, the 307th BG arrived to find the refinery shrouded by cloud cover. Seven of their twenty-three Liberators bombed by radar. Others dropped by 'dead reckoning' into the murk. When the 90th BG arrived, the target was totally blanketed and one squadron dropped its bombs. The 'Long Rangers', like the 'Bomber Barons' before them, were met by unexpectedly fierce fighter resistance, and three 5th BG Liberators were shot down.

It was the beginning of numerous trips to Balikpapan by FEAF. As noted earlier, Gen Kenney (who had asked in vain to be given B-29 Superfortresses for the 30 September 1944 strike) now commanded FEAF, which was responsible for both Fifth and Thirteenth Air Force – an arrangement similar to the US Strategic Air Forces in Europe (USAFE), though exercising more direct control. Seventh Air Force was to be added to FEAF's roster in the summer of 1945 and the Twentieth Air Force after the war.

On 3 October 1944 Balikpapan was the target again, and the 307th BG put 20 Liberators over the Pandansari refinery. Fighters swarmed around them and five Liberators were lost, vis-a-vis 19 fighters claimed. Some airmen began calling Balikpapan the 'Ploesti of the Pacific', referring to the Romanian oilfields hit by Liberators in their best-known combat action on 1 August 1943. Missions to Balikpapan continued, but the next time – and every time thereafter – fighter escort went along.

INDIES

To continue missions in the Indies, the 'Long Rangers' moved to Morotai in late 1944. Remembered Roger Ellis, an engineer with the 424th BS/307th BG, 'Morotai is that dot just east of the Celebes in the South Pacific. We were very frugal and only used one-half of the island. Bypassed Japanese soldiers had the other half. Australian troops on the perimeter strongly suggested to the Japanese that they adhere to the terms

A Royal Australian Air Force (RAAF) Liberator of No 21 Sqn, 82 Wing, passes over a wrecked Japanese aircraft at Labuan Island, on Borneo, during Allied landings at that sector of the Netherlands East Indies on 10 June 1944. No 21 Sqn was the RAAF's second operational Liberator unit, coming on strength in February 1944. The RAAF was asked to take on the duties of the 380th BG, which for two years had provided the main offensive strength in the north-western area, operating under Australian command (*via Allan G Blue*)

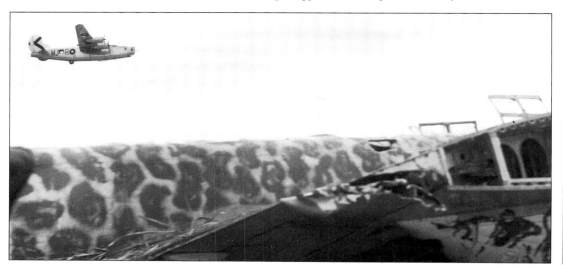

of their lease and not wander down towards our Pitoe airstrip. This did not preclude "Washing Machine Charlie" (so called because of his distinctive sounding engine) from night time visits and a bomb or two to send us to the fox holes.

'Things had quieted down in those last months of the war when we flew our missions. There was still flak over some targets but few fighter sightings – thank you very much! Our missions were meant to soften up Borneo for Allied invasion and close the faucet on the oil fields and refineries that the Japanese were using to fuel their war machine (especially Balikpapan).

Ellis remembered the 'fantastic view' observing the foe during a low-level strike. 'I looked back between the big rudders from the upper turret. We did a tree-top run at a Jap tanker in a river in Borneo. The whole world behind us turned black with boiling flame. I suppose George, our tail gunner, being even closer was even more impressed and had the same thought as I – "Wasn't that really a little too close?"

'There were enough goofs (mistakes) to go around in most crews. Like one of us that climbed down into the ball turret after we had to stop on the landing roll with a blown tyre. He let go a burst of .50-cal (12.7-mm) fire across the field when he hit the trigger accidentally. I wonder how the

A traffic jam forms around a 'cracked-up' PB4Y-1 Liberator of VD-5 in the Philippines on 10 March 1945 (*via Jim Sullivan*)

Seen from the starboard side earlier in this chapter, B-24J *"Shack Bunny"* of the 867th BS/494th BG was photographed flying over the Gulf of Davao en route to bomb Japanese installations around the Mintal airfield, a few miles west of the city of Davao on the Philippine island of Mindanao. The date is March 1945 (*via William Hess*)

B-24J-180-CO Liberator 44-40790 of the 867th BS/494th BG was part of a 25-bomber strike mounted from Anguar Island, in the Carolines, against the Licanan airfield, in the southern part of Mindanao, Philippines, on 19 February 1945. The raid was requested by friendly guerrilla troops near the target, who planned to mount a ground attack following the air strike (*via William Hess*)

A72-111 was an RAAF B-24L-15-CO Liberator (44-41663) transferred from the 380th BG 'Flying Circus' to Australian charge on 11 September 1944. Notes on the ultimate disposition of this airframe say that it did not fly after 12 June 1945, and was broken up after 12 March 1952 (*Pima Air and Space Museum*)

trigger could have been live after we shut down the aeroplane's systems. Was there a manual/mechanical trigger that would fire the guns with a kick of the foot?' Today, no one remembers.

PRIVATEERS

The first 'new' squadron to receive and deploy with single-tail PB4Y-2 Privateers was VPB-118. The unit left the 'States in November 1944 and was in the combat zone by about March 1945. VPB-106, meanwhile, was going out on a second tour and got new Privateers in the autumn of 1944. The PB4Y-2 – used only in the Pacific theatre during the war – introduced a new tail unit with a single fin, a lengthened forward fuselage, changes in armament to increase firepower to 12 .50-cal. (12.7-mm) machine guns and four Pratt & Whitney R-1830-94 Twin Wasp engines without superchargers.

The new squadrons that received the Privateer in 1944 were VPB-118, -119, -120, -121, -122, -123, -124 and -143. The returning squadrons that were re-equipped with Privateers and were on a second tour, or received Privateers on station, were VPB-101, -102, -104, -106, -108, -109, -111, -115, -116 and -117. Two training squadrons, VPB-197 (San Diego) and VPB-200 (Kaneohe Bay, Hawaii), also got Privateers in the

early training phases of the new bomber. A handful of RY-3 transports based on the Privateer were also operating in the Pacific region by war's end.

In addition to the Privateer, and for the identical purpose of replacing very war-weary B-24D/PB4Y-1 Liberators, many B-24Js were also delivered to the Navy. These too were designated PB4Y-1s, but had the ERCO bow turret in place of the Emerson turret in the nose. While the former looked exactly like the Privateer's ERCO bow turret externally, there were a few minor differences internally.

VB-102 and -104 made up the Navy Long Range Search Group, Solomons, and flew long and lonely missions against Japanese shipping. VB-106, with Cdr John 'Chick' Hayward as skipper, came to the South Pacific in November 1943 and ultimately sank or damaged 97 Japanese naval craft, including three submarines, while shooting down 20 fighters.

Like the Army's Liberators, the Navy's four-engined bombers marched north-east as the war against Japan turned toward the enemy's homeland. VPB-117 'Blue Raiders' was typical of the squadrons that fought from Guadalcanal to Leyte, flying long-range missions to support the October 1944 Leyte landings in the Philippines. The squadron flew from Biak and Morotai, then Tacloban, in the Philippines, before moving north to Tinian for the final fight against Japan itself.

Redesignated VPB-104 in accordance with changed Navy practice, the 'Buccaneers' began their second tour of duty in November 1944 under Cdr Whit Wright, operating from Tacloban airfield in the Philippines.

The diagonal fin stripe is the give-away that these Liberators hail from the 865th BS/494th BG. B-24M-15-CO 44-42056 leads a wingmate toward the target at Cebu, in the Philippines, on 25 March 1945. The wartime caption states that the target was Japanese installations in a partially wooded area six miles (about ten kilometres) west of Cebu city (*via William Hess*)

VPB-116 at Tinian began operating Privateers on long-reach missions against the Japanese homeland, whilst VPB-108 installed fixed 20 mm cannons in the noses of its Privateers and went after Japanese harbours, shipping and industrial sites. Twin-tailed Liberators remained in service with the US Navy well into 1945, including the PB4Y-1Ps of VD-5, which covered the February 1945 invasion of Iwo Jima.

Near war's end, Privateers began carrying the SWOD-9 Bat – a plywood glider shell encasing a 1000-lb (454-kg) bomb – singularly under each wing. Once dropped, the weapon was controlled from the Privateer until its internal radar locked onto the target. No structural modifications were required to the aircraft's wing in order to carry these glide bombs, but because of internal changes, the mother ship was redesignated PB4Y-2B. In April 1945 at Palawan, in the Philippines, VPB-109 became the first Bat-equipped squadron, and after a couple of tentative efforts, the unit employed the weapon successfully on 27 May 1945 when Lt Leo Kennedy sank a Japanese destroyer at sea – the missile blew the vessel's entire bow off.

On 31 May 1945 VPB-123 arrived at Tinian to relieve -109, with VPB-124 joining the fighting soon afterwards. These new squadrons made little attempt to exploit the Bat, however, which was plagued with reliability problems.

By July 1945 Privateers were well established at Yontan Field, Okinawa and on Tinian, while others (VPB-106 for example) were covering the Philippines from Palawan.

The RAAF's A72-75 was formerly B-24L-1-CO 44-41403, operated by the 380th BG. This bomber was brought on charge by the Australians on 16 October 1944, and the notes regarding the ultimate disposition of this airframe state that it did not fly after 26 November 1945 and was broken up after 12 March 1952 (*Pima Air and Space Museum*)

THE 20th CMS

The 20th CMS, with its F-7 Liberator photo-ships and *Yosemite Sam* cartoon character, moved from Nadzab, New Guinea, to Biak in September 1944. Later, the squadron flew from Dulag, Leyte, returned to Biak, then to Tacloban, Leyte, Clark Field and, in the final week of the war, Okinawa.

The 90th BG 'Jolly Rogers' moved to Biak on 10 August 1944. One of the Schouten Islands, Biak strategically lays across the entrance of Geelvink Bay, in north-western New Guinea. The island had been won with the blood of the 41st Infantry Division on 27 May 1944, followed soon after by the 24th Infantry Division. Biak was "probably the worst place I have ever been stationed', one B-24 crewman remembered. 'The

Japs ran wild during our entire stay there. We never felt safe. There was also an outbreak of hepatitis, called by us "Biak Bile". Another Liberator crew member recalled, 'These islands are truly "coral atolls". The "ground" where cleared was painfully white in the direct sun, and would take the torrential, near daily, rains with virtually no run-off. This allowed the Japs to honey-comb the bluffs above the invasion beach with caves'. This crewman added, "The (Norden) bombsight shop was the only – to my knowledge – air-conditioned facility on the Island (because) we didn't dare open a Norden sight in the prevalent high humidity'.

Another veteran, co-pilot 1Lt Phil Gowing, recalled what it was like to fly from the island;

'Here's what we did many times while flying 12 to 14 hour missions from Biak to Philippines and return for the 400th BS of the 90th BG. After take-off and reaching cruise altitude, we put the old war bird on AFCE and flew very loose formation (keeping the lead plane in sight) for four or five hours. The pilot, co-pilot, navigator, radio operator and engineer – all of us – were all fairly good bridge players. We would sit back in the navigator area and deal the cards. Whoever was dummy would adjust the auto pilot and throttles to keep the lead plane in sight. We had some great games, and all became fairly proficient in bridge. I know I left a lot of money in poker games, but I more than made it up in bridge. What a way to fight a war! We did get back to our stations during bomb runs and also during interception and/or ack-ack.'

Lady Eve **was a B-24J-170-CO Liberator (44-40647) of the 867th BS/494th BG, and it is seen flying over the Gulf of Davao, off Mindanao, en route to bomb Japanese installations in a Philippine village called Ising. The date was 24 February 1945, and this was one of many combat missions flown in direct support of friendly guerrilla forces in the Philippines (via William Hess)**

This B-24 was photographed taking off late in the war, with a row of single-fin PB4Y-2 Privateers parked off in the background (via Allan G Blue)

Throughout the 27 months between November 1942 and January 1945, the 90th BG was constantly in action flying very small (at times, as few as two aircraft) missions over very long distances (up to fifteen hours in the air). The group received a distinguished unit citation for strikes conducted through heavy flak and fighter opposition on Japanese airfields at Wewak, New Guinea, in September 1943. Other operations included participation in the Battle of the Bismarck Sea in May 1943 and long-range raids on oil refineries at Balikpapan, Borneo, in September and October 1944.

As the war moved toward Japan, the 90th BG went to San Jose, Mindoro, in the Philippines on 26 January 1945. The 'Jolly Rogers' supported ground forces on Luzon, attacked industries on Formosa and bombed railways, airfields and Harbor facilities on the Asiatic mainland.

7 FEBRUARY 1945

John Farrell was a pilot with the 90th BG's 319th BS 'Asterperious'. He took off from Mindoro in a B-24J on 7 February 1945 to bomb Tainan airfield on Formosa;

'I was leading the 319th – we were "tail end Charlie" so I was tucked up under the lead squadron as close as I could get. We expected intense ack-ack and plenty of fighters. Just as we neared the southern coast I noticed the puffs of ack-ack ahead of us.'

What Farrell didn't expect was to be nearly killed by an item of friendly equipment.

'Suddenly, the windshield broke and I was hit in the left shoulder. The air rushing through the windshield blinded me so I yelled for the co-pilot to take over. As I turned away and began to check myself out for wounds, I heard my navigator laughing.

'Turning toward the rear of the cockpit, I could see dozens of rolls of tin-foil scattered about the flight deck. Instead of throwing out the individual rolls to disturb the enemy radar, some idiot in one of the other planes had thrown out a full box. These weighed about 10 lb (4.5 kg), and were dense enough to go right through the windshield. Although I had a sore shoulder for a few days, I did not get a purple heart. Our crew went on to fly 60 missions without a scratch, nor was our plane ever severely damaged.'

B-24 Liberators of the 392nd BS/30th BG, Seventh Air Force, taxy out at the start of yet another mission. As the war pressed relentlessly closer to Japan, Seventh Air Force became part of the Far East Air Forces command, which already included Fifth and Thirteenth (*via Allan G Blue*)

The 'Jolly Rogers' transferred from the Philippines to Ie Shima on about 10 August 1945. After the move to Ie Shima – a postage stamp of an island just off Okinawa – the 90th BG ended the war flying reconnaissance missions over Japan, then ferried Allied prisoners from Okinawa to Manila.

HONG KONG

On 2 April 1945 the 90th and 380th BGs, in a combined operation, became the first Fifth Air Force units to raid mainland China when they struck the Japanese-occupied British colony at Hong Kong.

The primary target was shipping in the harbour as FEAF's Kenney wanted to clog the port with sunken wrecks. Docks and warehouses were secondary targets. The mission flew over an almost empty harbour and met with heavy AA. The 90th went for the Kowloon Docks, which were hit in bombing described by bombardier Lt James Blaisdell as the 'most beautiful group bombing I've seen'. One Liberator was hit by anti-aircraft fire but not badly damaged.

The 380th bombed the Taikoo Docks on Hong Kong Island with 1000-lb (454-kg) bombs with 'good results'. They were attacked by two Nakajima Ki-44 'Tojo' fighters from Kai Tak airfield, but these were driven off by escorting P-38s Lightnings. One B-24 nicknamed *PATCHES* lost an engine due to AA, and the captain landed at San Marcelino in Luzon.

ROYAL AUSTRALIAN AIR FORCE

Aside from the bomber's use with the various AAFs bomb groups in the Pacific, the B-24 also proved to be great success with the Royal Australian Air Force (RAAF). Nos 12, 21, 23, 24, 25, 99 and 102 Sqns all received Liberators, whilst Nos 200 and 201 Flights operated the big bomber as Special Duty units dropping resistance forces into the Dutch East Indies – the Australian equivalent of the European SOE. Even today, an

An H_2X radar 'thimble' protrudes from the ball-turret position of this B-24J Liberator of the 819th BS/30th BG, Seventh Air Force. These bombers are flying over Iwo Jima, which looks terribly small from above, but was large enough to claim the lives of 4000 Marines in one of the war's worst battles (*via Robert F Dorr*)

The Navy's PB4Y-2 Privateer was longer and heavier than the Liberator, with a distinguishing single-tail shape. Privateers began equipping VPB squadrons in 1944, subsequently becoming part of the war against the Japanese home islands (*Consolidated*)

Australian says, 'We are still trying to get their records declassified – like pushing water up hill with a fork'. A couple of C-87 Liberator transports were also operated.

The RAAF began receiving B-24Ds in 1943, and assigned serials beginning with A72. Numbers ultimately allocated were A71-1 to -13, A72-31 to -148 and A72-300 to -405. Most of these aircraft were B-24J, L- and M-models. Although much of the RAAF's combat operations with the Liberator were conducted over Burma, which, as part of the CBI (China-Burma-India) Theatre, falls outside the scope of this volume, some flying was also performed late in the war over the Indies.

The first such mission was performed by No 21 Sqn on 11 January 1945, and took the form of a 12-hour armed reconnaissance of Dutch islands west of Timor. Like many missions flown by Aussie pilots, this was eventless. Things were different in July 1945, however, when RAAF Liberators bombed the ubiquitous Balikpapan in preparation for a long-awaited Allied invasion – now there were flak and fighters to contend with.

No 24 Sqn also saw action in the Indies from Fenton, hitting targets in Java and Borneo. On one such raid on 6 April 1945, A72-77 was attacked by Japanese fighters and managed to shoot down an A6M2 'Hamp' before it, too, was blasted out of the sky. Five crewmen parachuted. Fighters also bagged a second Liberator in the form of A72-81, and again five men got out. In an added twist to these engagements, a Catalina that had rescued two of these flyers was then itself

Close-up of B-24J tail gun position (*via Dave Klaus*)

Nose art became ever more audacious as the war pressed on. *Pistol Pakin Mamma* was a Liberator flying from Kwajelein (*via William Hess*)

caught in the water and set afire. A running battle went on as a second Catalina arrived and got some of the flyers out.

Most RAAF Liberators survived the war but little further use was made of them and all had been officially disposed of by 1952.

TWENTIETH AF

The Twentieth Air Force, which used the hard-won Marianas Islands to mount the final offensive against the Japanese home islands – and later became part of FEAF – had a small number of Liberators that flew in the shadow of an armada of B-29 Superfortresses. According to the AAF Statistical Summary, the Twentieth AF received a total of 33 B-24s – 14 in 1944 and 19 during the period January-August 1945. One additional B-24 was lost in 1944 en route from the US.

As part of Twentieth, the 3rd Photo Recon Squadron operated primarily F-13A Superfortresses, but also had a small number of B-24 and F-7 Liberators that served as radar reconnaissance aircraft to chart the location of Japanese radar sets. The F-13As flew 427 sorties with six losses, but the contribution of the Liberators appears to be limited to 31 sorties.

Also attached to Twentieth was the 55th Reconnaissance Squadron (Long Range, Weather), equipped with B-24L/M Liberators. These 'Libs' carried out weather reconnaissance missions in support of the B-29 campaign against Japan. The 55th differed from almost every other squadron in the Pacific in that some of its Liberators were manufactured by Ford, in Dearborn. Most of these Liberators had caricatures or nicknames, but did not carry special markings, although a few had the squadron emblem on the tail.

LIBERATORS FOREVER

The final months of the war against Japan were dominated by the Twentieth Air Force's B-29 Superfortress. The most destructive bombing mission in history was a low-level incendiary attack by B-29s on Tokyo in March 1945 that ignited the hottest fires ever to burn on the earth. Japan had already been defeated by the time B-29s of the 509th BG took off on 6 August 1945 to drop the 'Little Boy' uranium weapon on Hiroshima, followed three days later by the 'Fat Man' plutonium bomb on Kokura. The latter mission was diverted by weather to another city –

PB4Y-1P Liberator BuNo 32143 of reconnaissance squadron VD-4, circa December 1944 (*via Tom McCarthy*)

Hulks of wrecked PB4Y-1 Liberators and a PB4Y-2 Privateer on Iwo Jima in July 1945. Just after the war, a surplus Liberator could be purchased by a private citizen for $18,000. Today, the price would be beyond measure (*Bill Derry via Jim Sullivan*)

Nagasaki – but long before then, the B-29 campaign, with some help from from the B-24 Liberator, had defeated Japan.

Perhaps to symbolise the role of the Consolidated bomber, Seventh Air Force B-24s were in action the day before and the day after Hiroshima. On 5 August they struck Tarumizu, where a factory was manufacturing the Kuguisho Okha 'Baka' rocket-propelled suicide aircraft. Two days later, 23 Liberators of the 11th BG struck the coal liquefaction plant at Omuta. On 11 August, in one of the final Liberator raids before the 15 August surrender, Liberators of the 11th and 494th BGs bombed Kurume and ignited fires that razed a quarter of the city.

Eight days prior to that, on the 7th, an 868th BS Liberator, *LADY LUCK II*, piloted by Lt E B Mills, had become the last 'Snooper' SB-24 to be lost in action, and the only American aeroplane to fall on Korean soil during the war. *LADY LUCK II* went down during a raid on the south-east coast of Korea, with the loss of all its crew.

The last Privateer lost in World War 2 was from VPB-121 in mid-August 1945 in a short encounter with several Japanese fighters. A second Privateer escaped with one engine out and one man wounded. The loss of Lt John Rainey's Privateer resulted in half the crew being killed and the survivors being captured and tortured in the closing days of the war. Despite this, the PoWs beat the squadron back to the US in September 1945.

It is unclear which was the first Liberator to land on the soil of a defeated Japan. On 2 September 1945, 1Lt Fred C Low of the 531st BS/380th BG put down at Atsugi in B-24M-15-FO 44-50927 *BATCHELORS BROTHEL* – one of possibly several claims to being the first Liberator in Japan.

With the end of the war, most AAF crews simply wanted to pack up and go home, but a few 'number-crunchers' toted up the score. They noted, for example, that 'Kelly's Cobras' of the 494th BG flew 5565 hours in combat prior to their first loss, and more than 10,000 altogether. From 2 November 1944 until 12 August 1945, the 494th mounted 146 B-24 missions, flying 3172 sorties with 6429 tons of bombs. Thirteenth Air Force bombers alone (B-24s and B-25s) had dropped 61,929 tons of bombs.

APPENDICES

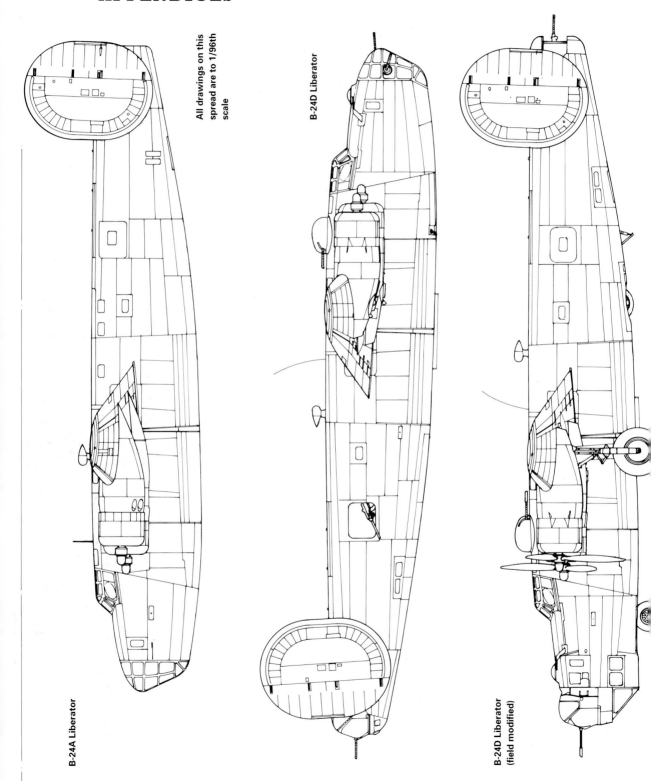

B-24A Liberator

All drawings on this spread are to 1/96th scale

B-24D Liberator

B-24D Liberator
(field modified)

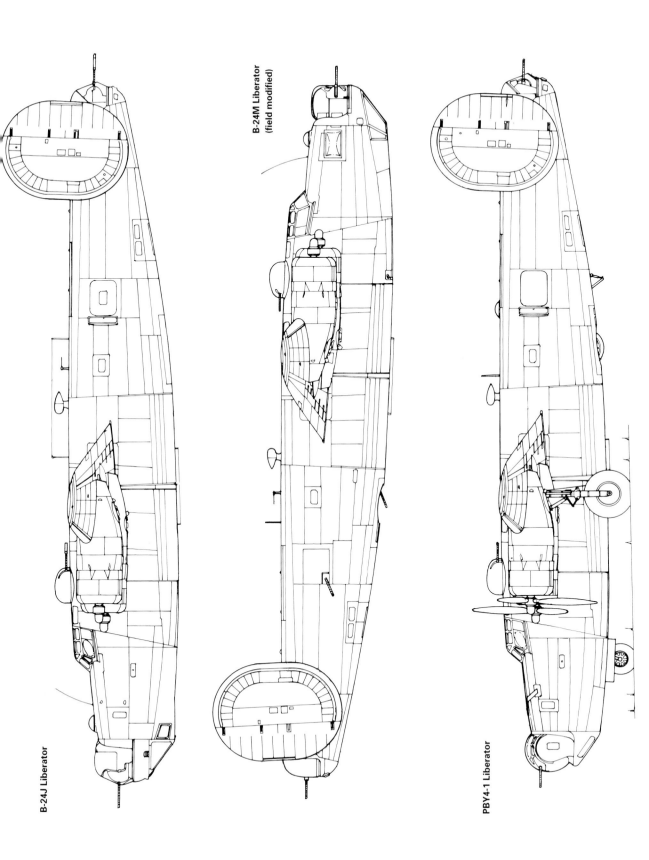

B-24J Liberator

**B-24M Liberator
(field modified)**

PBY4-1 Liberator

COLOUR PLATES

1

B-24A 40-2371 flown by 1Lt Ted Faulkner, 88th Reconnaissance Squadron, Pearl Harbor, 7 December 1941

This B-24A Liberator was intended for a photo project in the Pacific, although before it could undertake its mission it became the first US aircraft destroyed on the ground at Pearl Harbor on 7 December 1941. Only the final two digits of the serial number ('71') appeared on the fin of the aircraft, applied by Ferrying Command during the Liberator's earlier incarnation as a transport. The national insignia was the pre-war version, with a red circle in the centre of the US star. A crew member of Faulkner's aircraft remembers that the US flags on the nose and the top were still on the Liberator as of the time of the Pearl Harbor attack, even though they too were Ferrying Command markings. The B-24A had no nose painting or nickname. This B-24A was delivered to the AAF on 20 January 1941, and as of 30 November 1941 it had logged 173.8 flying hours. One of two B-24s despatched to Hawaii, 40-2371 took off on the night of 4 December 1941 for the Territory of Hawaii, and arrived early on the 5th. Both B-24As had earlier been despatched to the Sacramento (California) Air Depot on 26 November 1941 to make them ready for their mission. The bombers had been stripped of combat equipment by Ferrying Command during their brief tenure as transports (the job performed by other B-24As during the war), so much had to be done to make them war-ready. Not surprisingly, modifications were still incomplete when the first aircraft left Sacramento. Installation of camera equipment (details of which have not surfaced) at the Air Depot did not alter the B-24's external appearance.

2

LB-30 AL576 flown by 1Lt William Bayse, 11th BS/7th BG, Java, January 1942

This LB-30 Liberator typifies the early multi-engined AAF bombers that fought desperately on Java in January-February 1942. The 7th BG had two squadrons on the large Dutch-controlled island, namely the 9th with B-17E Flying Fortresses and the 11th with LB-30s. When Japan attacked Pearl Harbor, Bayse and the 11th BS were on the west coast of America preparing (they thought) to fly B-17Es to the Philippines. Instead, they went to Tucson, Arizona, and transitioned onto the LB-30. The unit's Liberators had left the Consolidated factory painted to the British contract specification, which was the standard RAF four-engined monoplane pattern executed in Dark Green (BS641/FS34079) and a deep brown colour the British termed 'Dark Earth' (BS450/FS30118) – undersurfaces were matt black (BS642/FS37038). As for AL576, this aircraft was delivered to the AAF in October 1941. After circling the globe to reach Java, it was lost in the 7th BG's first combat mission when, damaged by fire from Japanese A6M5 Zero fighters, Bayse crash-landed at Macassar, Celebes, on 16 January 1942. Only four of the twelve LB-30s which reached Java survived – one (AL608) went to India and three (AL508, AL515 and AL570) went to Australia. Of the remaining eight, seven (AL533, AL535, AL567, AL572, AL576, AL609 and AL612) were written off on the island, and one (AL521) was lost during an air raid on Darwin.

3

LB-30 AL640 *Jungle Queen* of the 397th BS/6th BG, Panama Canal Zone, 1942-43

AL640 was one of numerous Liberators built for British service, inducted into the AAF, and used to defend the Panama Canal. AL640 was delivered to the AAF on 6 January 1942 and eventually issued to the Sixth Air Force, who used it for punishing anti-submarine patrols over the Caribbean and Pacific prior to it being converted into a transport. The 397th BS/6th BG in Panama used the considerable talents of PFC William M Carter to paint many LB-30s and B-24s with nose art like that on *Jungle Queen*. This aircraft wore its female figure on both sides of the cockpit, with the pose reversed. AL640 served the 6th BG until 1 November 1943, when the group was disbanded.

4

B-24D-15-CO 41-24074 *Tokio Express* of the 319th BS/90th BG at Port Moresby, November 1942

This profile shows B-24D-15-CO 41-24074 early in the bomber's South Pacific career, the bomber having made its first flight at San Diego on 13 October 1942. Delivered to the AAF seven days later, it was flown out to Col Arthur Rogers' 90th BG soon afterwards. The premier Fifth Air Force B-24 outfit in-theatre, the 90th used 41-24074 in anger for the first time on 16 November 1942 when it bombed Buin-Faisi at Bougainville.

5

B-24D-7-CO 41-23849 *The EAGER BEAVER* flown by 1Lt Charles Whitlock, 320th BS/90th BG, Port Moresby, 1942-43

The EAGER BEAVER is typical of B-24Ds that made up the initial complement of the 90th BG 'Jolly Rogers' at Port Moresby, New Guinea. Construction of this aircraft began on 6 August 1942, and Consolidated completed it 14 days later. It was delivered to the AAF on 26 August, and unlike with many of its contemporaries, it was not modified with a B-24J-style nose turret. 1Lt Charles Whitlock, who was later a Dean at Harvard University after the war, became the pilot of *The EAGER BEAVER* after his initial Liberator, *LITTLE EVA*, was shot down on a mission (carrying *The EAGER BEAVER*'s initial pilot). Whitlock became a major within a short space of time, and was later made deputy group commander under Harry Bullis, who had in turn replaced Arthur Rogers as commander of the 'Jolly Rogers'. Part of the 320th BS, 41-23849's crew chief during its time in the frontline was Sgt Bernard Hanson. The bomber was also flown by Capt Wiley Wood, and, according to one source, was ultimately credited with having completed 77 missions, during which its crew downed three Zeroes and sunk three ships. *The EAGER BEAVER* returned to the USA in the fall of 1943 to be used in a war bond drive because of its many missions. Whitlock, having returned to America the following year, was participating in training evaluation when he saw a weary Liberator being stripped of paint in preparation for it use as an instructional aid. Upon checking its tail number he recognised it as *The EAGER BEAVER*.

6

B-24D-65-CO 42-40522 *DELIVERER* flown by 1Lt David T Brennan, 531st BS/380th BG, New Guinea, July 1943

42-40522 was brought to the war zone by 1Lt David T Brennan. Its crew chief during its time with the group was M/Sgt William W Baker, whilst its flight engineer, T/Sgt Francis Capraotta, chose its nickname, which was accompanied by a depiction of a bomb-carrying stork on both sides of the nose. This aircraft made its initial flight on 19 March 1943, and was delivered to the AAF in San Diego four days later. By 16 April *DELIVERER* was in Tucson for modification, and with the completion of its fitting out, it was flown to Hamilton Field, in California, on 22 April in preparation for it departure for Australia. This duly took place on 1 May, the bomber arriving in Brisbane seven days later. It was then quickly posted north to New Guinea, where it flew 33 missions with the 380th, accumulating 587.25 hours. Whilst with the 380th, *DELIVERER* was flown primarily by the crew of 1Lt David Brennan. Its most momentous mission was the Babo airfield strike on 10 July 1943. Nearing the target, the B-24s tangled with Ki-43 'Oscar' fighters of the transiting 59th Sentai, and after a chaotic series of manoeuvres which almost caused a collision with Lt Harold Merkel's *ESMERALDA II* (42-40507), an 'Oscar' attacked the latter bomber with such ferocity that its centre wing section disappeared in a blinding explosion. Parachutes were seen, but no record ever surfaced of any survivors. Raked by gunfire and 'immersed' in 'Oscars', Brennan pressed on to Babo despite having his tail gunner, S/Sgt Howard P Sachs, wounded by the Japanese fighters. The pilot managed to bomb the target and then fight his way out amid turbulence, gunfire and other bombers battling Ki-43s. A crewman seeking to assist Sachs was initially pounded about by the combative gunner, but the wounded crewman eventually calmed down after being given a shot of morphine and a cigarette. *DELIVERER* got home, Sachs lived and another gunner was so badly shaken up that he never flew again. The bomber was also involved in the historic missions by the 380th in August 1943 to Balikpapan, Borneo, flying in the night mission of the 16th. Its pilot on that mission was 531st BS Commander,

and later Group CO, Capt F L Brissey. Following months of near continual operations, *DELIVERER* was flown by Lt Carl D Magee's crew to Townsville from Long Strip, near Darwin, for a nose turret conversion and transfer to the RAAF, which was completed on 1 March 1944. The bomber was then assigned to the No 7 OTU (Operational Training Unit) on 1 May 1944 as A72-6. It survived the war and was broken up for parts in August 1947.

7

B-24D-65-CO 42-40489 *MISS GIVING* flown by 1Lt Jack R Banks, 528th BS/380th BG, Fenton, August 1943

One of the original bombers brought to Australia and later New Guinea by the 380th BG, 42-40489 was initially assigned to 1Lt Jack R Banks, who had a reputation for being 'bait' for Japanese fighters. This aircraft was a standard D-model (without a nose turret), attired in olive drab with light under-fuselage and lower wing surfaces. It made its first flight on 13 March 1943 and was delivered to the AAF four days later. *MISS GIVING* participated in many of the 'Flying Circus's'' early long-range sorties, going to Surabaya and Macassar. On a post-strike reconnaissance mission to Balikpapan on 15 August 1943, Banks' gunners were credited with shooting down four Zero fighters before the B-24 returned to its base at Fenton. Two more kills came later, one of them being a Ki-45 Toryu, or 'Nick'. After 26 missions and six kills, *MISS GIVING* was sent to Townsville in February 1944, where it was refurbished and transferred to the RAAF as A72-4. It was damaged in a fire at Tocumwal, New South Wales, in October 1944, but nevertheless survived the war and was struck off RAAF charge in June 1950.

8

B-24J-15-CO 42-73155 *Tired Tessie* flown by 1Lt J Snyder, 431st BS/11th BG, Funafuti, late 1943

This aircraft made its first flight on 16 September 1943 and was delivered to the AAF four days later. The 11th BG began the war in the South Pacific operating B-17 Flying Fortresses with Thirteenth Air Force. In early 1943 the group transferred to Seventh Air Force in the central Pacific and began flying olive drab Liberators. By late 1943, B-24s of the 11th and companion 30th BG had an aircraft number painted on either side of the nose in yellow. Liberators in both groups also adopted squadron symbols on their vertical tails – in the 11th BG, these took the form of a triangle (26th BS), a square (42nd BS), three horizontal stripes (98th BS) and three vertical yellow stripes (431st BS), reported incorrectly in one source to have been white. The crew of *Tired Tessie*, led by 1Lt John Snyder, with 1Lt Kevin Mendenhall as his co-pilot, was often accompanied on missions by 'PFC Merkatroid', the crew's canine mascot. A Yagi antenna for the radar can be seen beneath the co-pilot's window, a similar array being found on the port side of the aircraft. A forward-looking only system that had a notoriously cantankerous cath-

ode ray tube for the operator, Yagi was vividly
remembered by Liberator veteran Jim Harvill; 'On
the scope you had a centre line that ran from the
bottom to the top of the screen. Any projections to
one side or the other were targets. The distance
from the bottom of the screen was the range. It
took a good operator to interpret the screen, as the
centre line was always messed us with hash. The
same sort of thing you saw as ground return on
later radar. But the system worked okay if the
operator was good. And in the Pacific where targets were lonely, it was helpful to have'.

9

**PB4Y-1 BuNo 32081 *WHITSSHITS* flown by VB-104
XO, Cdr Whit Wright, Guadalcanal, late 1943**
B-24D-90-CO Liberator 52-40726 was delivered to
the US Navy as PB4Y-1 BuNo 32081, retaining the
olive-drab upper surfaces found on AAF bombers.
This aircraft made its maiden flight on 28 April
1943 and was delivered to the AAF on two days
later. As *WHITSSHITS*, it was flown by Cdr Whit
Wright when he was executive officer of VB-104
'Buccaneers' during the unit's first combat 'cruise'.
He later commanded the squadron (all VB
squadrons were redesignated as VPB squadrons
on 30 September 1944) at Tacloban airfield, in the
Philippines, during its second 'cruise', beginning in
November 1944. *WHITSSHITS* differs from B-24Ds
and early PB4Y-1s in having a nose-mounted Erco
250 SH ball turret with two .50-cal. (12.7-mm)
guns. The aircraft also has Yagi antenna protruding from beneath both pilots' windows.

10

**B-24D-170-CO 42-72963 of the 42nd BS/11th BG,
Funafuti, November 1943**
The last D-model manufactured in San Diego by
Consolidated, 42-72963 flew for the first time on 21
August 1943. It was delivered to the AAF four days
later, and upon its arrival in the central Pacific, it
was modified by the Hawaiian Air Depot through
the fitment of a Consair A-6 turret in the nose –
note the unusual nose window configuration. The
tail number is presented in white letters much
larger than its contemporaries. This B-24 enjoyed a
very brief frontline career, for after completing its
first mission with the 42nd BS on 21 November
1943 (to Nauru), it failed to return to Funafuti from
its next sortie on 1 December – 2Lt George R
Dechert and crew were listed as killed in action.

11

**B-24J-160-CO 42-109984 *"SHOO-SHOO BABY"* of
the 408th BS/22nd BG, Nadzab, February 1944**
"SHOO-SHOO BABY" was part of the 22nd BG,
which was one of the few bomb groups that took
the B-24 on charge after flying another aircraft
type in combat. 42-109984 made its first flight on
24 January 1944 and was delivered to the AAF
three days later. Its eventual disposition is not
known. The 22nd BG flew the B-26B and later the
B-25D prior to January 1944, when it converted to
B-24J/Ls and adopted the name 'Red Raiders'. This

aircraft was typical of the early olive-drab B-24s
flown by the 408th BS, which was distinguished
within the group by a green square on the fin.

12

**F-7A 42-64047 *PATCHED UP PIECE* of the 20th
CMS, Morotai, 14 August 1944**
This aircraft began life as the first B-24J-1-CF manufactured in Fort Worth, making its first flight on
14 September 1943 and being delivered to the AAF
on 2 October. When modified with cameras and
equipment for the reconnaissance mission, it
became the first of 43 F-7A reconnaissance aircraft
(which followed one XF-7 prototype and four F-7s),
and is depicted as it appeared during a difficult
mission from Morotai on 14 August 1944.
PATCHED UP PIECE apparently wore no national
insignia on its fuselage, whilst the nose art was
done by Al Merkling, who was considered to be an
artistic genius for his work on B-24s.

13

**B-24D-155-CO 42-72783 *Heather Angel* of the
372nd BS/307th BG, Noemfoor, September 1944**
This aircraft boasted a B-24J-style nose turret,
standard camouflage with some weathering and
the late-war national insignia adopted in
September 1943. 42-72783 made its first flight on
24 July 1943, and was delivered to the AAF six
days later. The B-24 survived long enough in the
frontline to take part in the fabled Thirteenth Air
Force raid on the Balikpapan oil refineries on 30
September 1944. The left waist-gun position displays three Japanese flags, indicating fighter 'kills'
with which various gunners had been credited.

14

**B-24J-165-CO 44-40532 *NIGHT MISSION* flown by
1Lt Winton E Newcomb, 819th BS/30th BG,
Saipan, October 1944**
The crew named this Liberator in the hope that
they would draw a nocturnal assignment, which
they considered less risky than a daytime bombing
raid. Despite the fact that they did not succeed in
their quest, *NIGHT MISSION* nevertheless completed 44 combat sorties with the 30th BG, plus
additional missions with the 11th BG. This aircraft
had previously made its first flight on 13 April 1944
and was delivered to the AAF at San Diego six
days later. On 24 September 1944, *NIGHT MIS-
SION* participated in an especially gruelling mission when ten B-24s bombed facilities at Chichi
Jima, in the Bonin Islands. 1Lt Winton E Newcomb
was the pilot of 44-40532 on this occasion, the aircraft being the last bomber to arrive at the target.
He made his bombing run at less than 50 ft (152
m) and sustained heavy flak damage. With two
men wounded and the rudder seriously damaged,
Newcomb struggled 800 miles (1287 km) to
Saipan, where he succeeded in pulling off a
remarkably difficult landing on the island airstrip.

15

SB-24J-85-CO 42-100271 'Snooper' *Lady June* of

the 868th BS, Noemfoor, 19 October 1944

42-100271 was on Consolidated's San Diego assembly line between 2-8 December 1943 and made its shakedown flight five days later, with a check flight on the same day. It was accepted by the AAF on the 14th and delivered on the 16th. When 1Lt Gordon Zwirtz took over this aircraft more than a year later, the caricature of a young woman was already painted on the nose – no record survives as to who named the aircraft. The bathing beauty was attired in a light blue one-piece swim suit, but may have appeared previously in the nude. Navigator Clayton Seavers was one of *Lady June*'s crew, and it was research by a member of Seavers' family that unearthed details on the colours and markings of this Liberator. Used for low-level night operations, this SB-24J 'Snooper' carried an SRC-717-B search and navigation radome resembling an upside-down thimble in the ventral location occupied by a ball turret. The 868th 'Snoopers' (originally the 394th BS/5th BG on Guadalcanal) covered vast distances from the south-west Pacific to the doorstep of Japan, operating from Munda, New Georgia, Los Negros, Noemfoor, Morotai, Leyte and Okinawa.

16

B-24D -160-CO 42-72815 *"SKY WITCH"* flown by Capt J J Ryan, 400th BS/90th BG, Mokmer airstrip, Biak, November 1944

This Liberator wears standard 'OD' camouflage, and has been modified with a B-24J-style nose turret. Internally, the aircraft had been specially equipped for long-distance photo and visual reconnaissance through the fitment of four additional four 400 US-gal bomb bay fuel tanks and two 160 US-gal auxiliary fuel tanks on the command deck. 42-72815 came off the San Diego production line on 28 July 1942, made its first shakedown flight 48 hours later, and was delivered on 2 August. It later became one of the early B-24Ds to go to war with the 'Jolly Rogers' in late 1942. Two years later, with Capt J J Ryan as pilot and 1Lt Phil Gowing as co-pilot, *SKY WITCH* set forth on 7 November 1944 to search for an expected Japanese fleet in Brunei Bay, off Borneo, days after the Battle of the Philippine Sea. The B-24D fought a continuous 40-minute battle with at least nine A6M5 Zeroes during the sortie, the Liberator's gunners being credited with downing four of them. Having fought itself clear of the fighters, *"SKY WITCH"* flew more than 1000 miles to friendly territory with photos and other intelligence, but was so battered from the engagement that it never flew again. 'It was junk after that', Gowing remembers. Crew members included: Sid Machtinger, navigator; Al Wright, flight engineer; Gene Sullivan, radio operator; and Bill Kubia, Ernie Rearick, Mike Edwards and Oley Schwichtenberg, gunners.

17

B-24J-165-CO 44-40526 *"Bat Out of Hell"* of the 819th BS/30th BG, Saipan, late 1944

44-40526 made its first flight from San Diego on 12 April 1944 and was delivered to the AAF six days later. It has a Consair A-6 nose turret – characteristic of B-24J-1-CO 42-72964 through to B-24J-180-CO 44-40848 and B-24J-1-CF 42-64047 through to B-24J-40-CF 44-10374, with the exception of the 57 airframes bearing serials 42-50452 through 42-50508. All other nose-turreted B-24s had the Emerson A15 mounting fitted. Records on the disposition of 30th BG B-24s have not yet surfaced.

18

PB4Y-1 BuNo 38892 *LADY LUCK* of Lt Cdr J V Barry, VPB-111, late 1944

This aircraft belonged to the commander of VPB-111 in late 1944, whilst Lt Cdr J V Barry was the 'PPC'. The PBY4-1 also carried the AAF serial 44-41279. It flew for the first time on 10 July 1944, and was delivered to the Navy eight days later.

19

B-24L-5-CO A72-84 (formerly 44-41456) *Cock o' the North*, No 24 Sqn, RAAF, Fenton, late 1944

This aircraft was delivered to the RAAF in October 1944, and following limited frontline service in the last months of the war, it became one of dozens of Liberators that remained 'on charge' until finally struck in December 1952. 44-41456 first flew on 5 August 1944, and was flown later that day to the Consolidated facility at Tucson, Arizona, where it was accepted by the AAF on 21 September 1944. No fewer than 287 Liberators were delivered to the RAAF between February 1944 and August 1945, including 12 B-24Ds, 145 B-24Js, 83 B-24Ls and 47 B-24Ms. The first four-engined bomber to see service from Australian soil, the Liberator served with Nos 12, 21, 23, 24, 25, 99 and 102 Sqns. Their wartime service was especially noteworthy during the Borneo campaign. No 24 Sqn became the first to use Liberators, replacing Vultee Vengeance dive-bombers that were deemed unsuitable for further operations. The unit's first operational mission was a supply drop in western New Guinea on 6 July 1944. *Cock o' the North* was operational with the RAAF by late 1944.

20

B-24J-170-CO 44-40604 *KIT'S TADGER* of the 371st BS/307th BG, McGuire's Field, Mindoro, the Philippines, January 1945

This B-24 first flew on 21 April 1944 and was delivered to the AAF four days later. On 24 January 1945 the *TADGER* suffered a direct flak hit to its ball turret near Manila, ripping the mounting away from the underside of the bomber and leaving the body of the dead gunner hung up in the debris until it eventually fell away into the sea. The aircraft subsequently recovered safely at Mindoro.

21

B-24J-150-CO 44-40193 *BOOBY TRAP* flown by Squadron Commander, Maj Stanley P Robeck, 321st BS/90th BG, McGuire Field, Mindoro, the Philippines, February 1945

This aircraft is typical of natural-metal B-24s flown

by the 'Jolly Rogers' in the last year of the war. *BOOBY TRAP* operated from McGuire Field, which the 90th BG shared with the 380th BG 'Flying Circus'. These markings are well known, but less familiar to most is the fact that the 'Jolly Rogers' also had an A-20 and a C-47 with the same fin emblem – the skull and crossed bombs. The crew of *BOOBY TRAP* was as follows: Maj Stanley P Robeck, unit commander; 2Lt Richard J Thurber, pilot; 2Lt James D Pierce, co-pilot 2Lt John E Wise Jr, navigator; 2Lt Irving Weinberg, bombardier; T/Sgt Leon E Lins, engineer; T/Sgt George J Erickson, radio operator; S/Sgt Howard V Canery, gunner; S/Sgt Kenneth A Johnson, gunner; S/Sgt George R Rothenberger, gunner; and S/Sgt James A Bregory, gunner. The unit commander flew the aircraft on a mission that resulted in a shaky landing at Mindoro after flak damage. 44-40193 had made its first flight on 6 March 1944, and was delivered to the AAF at San Diego 48 hours later.

22
B-24J-180-CO 44-40759 *Shack Bunny* of the 867th BS/494th BG, Angaur, March 1945
This aircraft wears the distinctive quartered black squares of the 494th BG's 867th BS, the unit fighting in the Philippines until it moved to Yontan, Okinawa, in June 1945. *Shack Bunny* first flew on 9 May 1944 and was delivered to the AAF three days later. Its final disposition is not on record.

23
B-24J-10-CO 42-73114 *CARROT TOP* of the 528th BS/380th BG, McGuire Field, Mindoro, the Philippines, March 1945
This bomber first flew on 11 September 1943 and was delivered to the AAF five days later. Devoid of a nickname, the bomber flew its first mission to Balikpapan on 10 December 1943. Research by Glenn Horton indicates that this Liberator flew 27 missions, one of its regular pilots being 1Lt Otto H Martens until his death on 19 March 1944. 1Lt Sherwood H. Sheehan then became *CARROT TOP's* pilot, and it was he who chose the nickname in honour of his redheaded wife, Norma – the artwork was drawn by gunner S/Sgt Eugene F Buck. During its combat duty, *CARROT TOP* was credited with the destruction of a Zero downed on just its second mission, to Kendari, on 8 January 1944. The veteran bomber eventually crashed and burned near Mindoro on 6 March 1945.

24
B-24M-30-FO 44-51589 of the 29th BS, Galapagos Islands, April 1945
Ford-built B-24M-30-FO 44-51589 was devoid of unit insignia or individual artistry when it flew with the 29th BS from the Galapagos Islands in April 1945. This bomber wore the distinctive 'patrol' scheme that cloaked several of the late-war B-24s used on gruelling anti-submarine patrols in defence of the Panama Canal. The '-FO' suffix of the bomber's designation indicates that the B-24 was built by Ford in Willow Run, Michigan, which was responsible for 6792 of the 19,256 Liberators and Privateers built. Other suffixes were: '-CO' for Consolidated in San Diego, California (7500); '-CF' for Consolidated in Fort Worth, Texas (3034); '-DT' for Douglas in Tulsa, Oklahoma (964); and '-NT' for North American in Dallas, Texas (966).

25
B-24M-20-CO 44-42246 of the 65th BS/43rd BG, Clark Field, Luzon, the Philippines, May 1945
This aircraft made its first flight on 26 January 1945, and as the AAF was no longer taking deliveries in San Diego, 44-42246 was delivered instead to Tucson on 19 February 1945. It was in turn issued to the 43rd BG, who were universally known with AAF as 'Ken's Men', in honour of Gen George C Kenney. The group initially operated B-17E/F Flying Fortresses, but began flying Liberators in May 1943. In his memoirs, Gen Kenney described how a squadron member told him about the nickname: 'Bill Benn came over for a chat. He said the 43rd Group wanted to call themselves the "Ken's Men", and did I have any objection. I told him that I had none, and to tell the gang that I felt highly honoured. The next time I inspected the group they had painted out the cute, scantily-clothed girls and substituted the words "Ken's Men" in block letters a foot high. I was flattered, of course, but I sort of missed the pretty gals'. The 65th BS, which began receiving aircraft in natural metal finish early on, applied a disc to the fins of its Liberators, inside of which was painted a pair of dice showing a '4' and a '3' to correspond to the group designation. Additionally, some, but not all, rudders were painted with three stripes. Jim Cherkhauer remembers the aircraft: 'I flew it two times in May 1945 from Clark Field, Philippines. On 9 May I flew the plane on a mission to Tien Ho Airdrome, Canton, China. On 23 May I flew the ship on a practice bombing mission out of Clark. We were developing new types of formations and needed to practice H_2X bombing. This was a form of radar guided bombing. My diary says that our bombs were about 6 ft (2 m) off target. That is darn good, but I have no idea today at what altitude we were dropping the bombs. I would guess it would be about 10,000-14,000 ft, as that was our normal altitude for our daily bombings of targets. Although it was a practice mission, we flew for six hours and were fired at by our own Navy as we flew down the west coast of Luzon. The plane had no nose art. I believe that it had no nose art at the end of the war either. The M- and L-models were really sweet planes to pilot. Most of our Js were getting quite war weary at that time, and some were much more difficult to handle under certain conditions'. Turning to the aircraft itself, the M-model lacked the 'tunnel gun windows' found on the lower rear of the J, whilst the small rectangular window on the nose of the B-24M took the form of a three-dimensional dome.

26
B-24M-1-CO 44-41809 *"Out Of The Night II"* of the

63rd BS/43rd BG, Clark Field, Luzon, the Philippines, 19 May 1945

The 63rd was known as the 'Sea Hawks' (note the emblem on the bomber's fin). AAF experiments showed that a gloss black finish was better than matte for night concealment, so the former was used. 44-41809 (the third M-CO produced) first flew on 28 September 1944. At this juncture, San Diego-built aircraft were being flown from the factory to Tucson to go through the modification process before delivery to the AAF. This aircraft flew to Tucson on 28 September 1944 and was delivered on 18 November. The Liberator served as a radar countermeasures (RCM), or 'ferret', aircraft, its mission equipment including two 'auto scan' receivers, a pulse analyser CRT (cathode ray tube), a Hewlett-Packard variable-frequency audio oscillator for precise determination of a radar pulse recurrence frequency (PRF) and antenna systems including an omni directional antenna for radar signal search. The only thing visible on the aircraft in profile is the radar antenna on the right side of the nose. The purpose of the 'ferret' missions was to detect and locate Japanese radar stations of interest to FEAF, including flight routes to and from such areas. In addition to fixing the location of the radar site, an important objective was to determine the radar's capabilities – particularly the detection range of the target as a function of the altitude and azimuth bearing. Apart from their radar 'ferret' role, the 'Sea Hawks' of the 63rd BS also employed their Liberators on night strikes against Japanese shipping and land targets.

27

B-24J-160-CO 44-40429 *MICHIGAN* of the 64th BS/43rd BG, Clark Field, Luzon, the Philippines, July 1945

44-40429 completed its maiden flight on 31 March 1944 and was delivered to the AAF on 4 April. The nose art on *MICHIGAN* was done by the same artist who decorated *THE DRAGON AND HIS TAIL* – a man named Bartigan, about whom no other details seem to have survived. He was famous for the way his paint brush made good use of the deep slab sides of the Liberator's nose. The reference, of course, is to the University of Michigan at Ann Arbor, and never, never to Michigan State. As a Pacific B-24 pilot remembered 53 years later, 'The Michigan colours are maize (corn yellow) and a dark blue, almost Navy. They have the ugliest helmets in all college football. Watch the sports sections for a few Sundays now that football is coming up (this volume was written in September 1998). You are sure to see some colour pics of those Godawful helmets real soon. Most of the nation's sportswriters are very enamoured of this team'. Some things never change.

28

B-24J-190-CO 44-40973 *THE DRAGON AND HIS TAIL* of the 64th BS/43rd BG, Ie Shima, mid-1945

This astoundingly marked B-24 is considered to have one of the most colourful crew insignia of all time. 44-40973 first flew on 3 June 1944 and was delivered to the AAF several days later. *THE DRAGON* flew for much of its combat career wearing this gaudy, glorious paint scheme. Its base was Ie Shima, described by one crew member as 'a lump of coral in the Bonins'. The artist who created this masterpiece was named Bartigan, who made himself famous (as well as possibly well-heeled) by creating fuselage-length murals on the 43rd BG's Liberators. Unfortunately, what is often credited as the most colourful aircraft of the war did not survive for preservation. *THE DRAGON* was last seen at Kingman, Arizona (one of the Reconstruction Finance Corporation's centres) postwar, where it apparently went to the smelter.

29

PB4Y-2 BuNo 59406 of VD-1, Guam, 1945

As compared with the twin-tailed Liberator, the PB4Y-2 had a 7-ft (2.13-m) extension added to the forward fuselage to accommodate a flight engineer's station and a single tall vertical tail which increased the height of the aircraft to 29 ft $1^{5}/8$ in (8.90 m). It was powered by four lighter 1200-hp Pratt & Whitney R-1830-94 radial engines without turbochargers in re-designed nacelles, with different-sized oil cooler scoops located above and below the nacelle rather than on the sides as in the B-24. The top inlet was for carburettor air, whilst the bottom served the oil cooler and heat exchanger. Production aircraft mounted a nose Erco 250 SH ball turret. The PB4Y-2 was built with two spine-mounted Martin A-3D dorsal turrets and two waist positions with Erco 250 THE tear-shaped blisters each housing a powered ball turrets. Radar and radar countermeasures bulges under the nose gave the impression that the Privateer had grown 'warts'. This PB4Y-2 had narrow-blade propellers, not the paddle-blade type. Although the AAF tested single-fin XB-24K/Ns, only the Navy ordered the Privateer and used it in combat, beginning in January 1945. With more speed and range, Privateer crews felt emboldened to go where Liberator crews had not. Their campaign against Japanese shipping and other targets was extremely effective, and produced relatively low casualties.

30

B-24M-30-CO 44-42418 *"Miss Ileene"* of the 23rd BS/5th BG, Samar, the Philippines, 1945

This bomber's nickname is given incorrectly as *"Miss Ileen"* in at least two published references. A late-build B-24, it made its maiden flight in San Diego on 1 March 1945 and was then flown to the Consolidated centre at Tucson 24 hours later. At the latter location, it was accepted by the AAF on 2 April 1945. The aircraft survived the war.

FIGURE PLATES

1

T/Sgt Robert O Spindler, radio operator with the 64th BS/43rd BG, Fifth Air Force, at Port Moresby,

New Guinea, in February 1944. He was part of the ten-man crew headed by H J 'Hank' Domagalski that flew 65 combat missions using whatever Liberator happened to be available on the day of the sortie. Spindler is wearing the standard long-sleeve worsted khaki uniform. Sewn onto the upper left sleeve of the shirt is the 'Streaking Comet' patch of the Fifth Air Force, whilst pinned above the left breast pocket is his aircrew wing badge. This is slightly off-centre so as not to interfere with his russet leather M-3 shoulder-holster, containing a Colt .45 service automatic without a clip installed. This piece of equipment was widely issued to aircrew, as its compact design enabled it to be worn comfortably beneath layers of flight clothing, and provided a means of self-defence in the event of a bail-out or forced landing behind enemy lines. Spindler is well-equipped for just such an eventuality, as he also carries a survival knife, suspended in its scabbard from his officer's pattern web-belt, with its plate-brass roller buckle. His footwear consists of the regulation GI service shoe in its 'rough side out' configuration, whilst his trousers are rolled-up 'chinos'.

2

Maj Austin Straubel, commander of the 11th BS (Heavy) within the 7th BG on Java in January 1942, is wearing the regulation Army/AAF summer uniform, which comprises a cotton khaki (shade number 1) shirt, pants and garrison overseas cap. This basic uniform was widely worn by all ranks throughout the Pacific campaign. As he is an officer, Straubel's shirt has shoulder loops, which was a feature not present on enlisted mens' shirts. Note that his insignia of rank (gold oak leaves) is displayed on his shoulder loops, this practice being abandoned in August of 1942 when revised regulations stated that, henceforth, insignia of rank was to be worn on the right collar in place of the 'US' block letters which had previously occupied this space. Visible on Straubel's left collar is the gold/silver winged-prop device of the AAF. Curiously, his rank insignia is not displayed on the left front of his garrison cap as per regulations. Pinned above the left breast pocket are his silver pilot's qualification wings. These appear to be the full three-inch size, although a smaller two-inch size was authorised for wearing on shirts. For personal protection, the major carries a standard Colt .45 M1911 A1 automatic pistol in its russet brown M-1916 leather holster, suspended from an M-1936 web pistol belt. The twin magazine pouch secured to the front left of his belt is of World War 1 vintage, due to the 'puckered' style of stitching along its lower edge. Finally, he is carrying a khaki canvas map/dispatch case, which was an essential item for all AAF pilots and navigators.

3

1Lt John F Lance was a pilot with the 23rd BS/5th BG, Thirteenth Air Force, at Morotai in November 1944. He is shown in his classic US Army/AAF officers' dress Class A uniform, popularly known as 'pinks and greens' because of the distinctive hues of the pants and jacket, respectively, when seen in bright sunlight. His dark olive drab (shade 51) service hat features the un-stiffened soft crown which was *de riguer* for all AAF officers. Russet leather, low-quarter, shoes of the regulation pattern are worn with this uniform. Above Lance's left breast pocket are his silver wings. The lack of ribbons beneath them suggests that this artwork features him early in his operational career. Matched pairs of 'US' block letters and AAF winged-prop devices are worn on the collar and lapels of the jacket in regulation fashion, whilst his lieutnant's bars are pinned to the shoulder loops, $5/8$ths of an inch from the shoulder seam. Finally, the familiar winged-star patch of the AAF is worn on the upper left sleeve. This generic patch was usually replaced by a specific numbered patch once an airman was assigned to one of the active air forces.

4

S/Sgt William L Adair was a gunner with the 23rd BS/5th BG, Thirteenth Air Force, at Morotai in November 1944. Although crews usually wore no special clothing when flying from tropical locations at low altitude in warm weather, even in the Pacific they sometimes flew at high altitude where it was always cold. Adair is seen wearing a ubiquitous A-2 leather flying jacket, beneath which he has on a regulation 'o.d.' woollen shirt and pants, which would be much warmer than the usual 'chinos' at altitude. As most Pacific flights involved long water crossings, Adair wears a B-3 Mae West as part of his basic equipment. In his hand he is holding a type A-3 quick-attachable chest-type parachute, with its distinctive red rip-cord pull handle. The shearing-lined flying helmet is a type B-6, with its ANB-H-1 receivers held in place by foam-rubber ear-cups. Attached to the helmet's snaps is an A-14 oxygen mask. Adair's footwear comprises a pair of russet brown GI service shoes.

5

Maj Gen Willis Hale, commander Seventh Air Force, is wearing regulation AAF officers' summer/tropical uniform, but given his rank, this invariably would have been privately-procured, and of superior quality. Interestingly, the general has opted to wear a dark olive drab service cap rather than its khaki equivalent, which would be the norm with such a uniform. Insignia is kept to minimum, with only the pairs of silver stars of his rank and his pilot's wings being worn.

6

This first lieutenant navigator at Townsville, in Queensland, Australia, in 1942 wears a B-3 shearling flying jacket over an A-4 flight suit. The former was finished in a deep brown waterproof laquer which was prone to cracking and crazing with wear and tear, thus earning these jackets the affectionate nickname 'Crusties'. A single lieutnant's silver bar is worn at the left front of his garrison cap, whilst his sunglasses are non-regulation.